The Feng Shui Advantage;

Get Your Space Working for YOU!

The Feng Shui Advantage

~Get Your Space Working for You!

By Kathryn Wilking

The Feng Shui Advantage

Copyright © 2023 by Kathryn Wilking

All rights reserved. No parts of this book may be used or reproduced by any means, graphic, electronic, and mechanical, including photocopying, recording, taping, or by any information storage retrieval system, without the written permission of the publisher except in the case of brief quotations embodied in critical articles and reviews.

ISBN: 978-1-961677-00-5 (Paperback)
ISBN: 978-1-961677-01-2 (E-book)
ISBN: 978-1-961677-45-6 (Hardback)

Library of Congress Control Number:

Printed in the United States of America

Published by Quippy Quill LLC

Acknowledgements

The reason this book is available is because I have people who support my vision to help others. My husband, Stephen Rigbey, still gets the prize for being the most patient, understanding and open-minded individual. He has been tolerant through all the rants and all the discussions about Feng Shui, human behaviour, office politics, EMFs and this book.

In the last few years, we've driven ourselves and the dog(s) across the country, and back. We moved three times in three years, executed enormous renovation(s), and we can still laugh together as we discuss the idiosyncrasies of life.

Yes, he 'gets' me and understands my quest to help change the world.

Yes, I believe if we all work together, we CAN make the world a better place. Enjoy the journey through life, wherever it takes you.

~~~

Every new adventure challenges me to be a better person.

~ Kathryn

Kathryn Wilking

Contents

Acknowledgements i

Forward: Working at Home, or is it *Living at Work?* v

Introduction to Feng Shui A Little History vii

1   Feng Shui Your Cubicle 1
Setting Goals, The Power Position, Work Stations, Choosing your desk and chair, Clutter

    The Meeting: Where Do I Need to Sit? 13

    ZOOM Etiquette Camera on face, Background, When to turn off 15

    At the Coffee Shop 19

2   Inside the Home Working from home, Cultivating the flow 23

    Working in Common Areas 25

    Supportive Décor 31

3   The Tool Box 35

    The Bagua Grid 35

    The Five Elements 42

    Combining these tools 44

4   The PEP Quiz: Personal Element Profile 59

    In Your Element Wood, Fire Earth, Metal and Water people 63

    Me: In My Element 86

5   Clues to Understand People 87

    Clutter Habit Clutter Game Clues 88

    Communications for Solving Problems Where to Tread Lightly 93

6   The Cycles of the Five Elements 99

    The Productive and Growth Cycle 101

    The Recovery Cycle 104

	The Cycle of Aggressive Behaviour 107
7	**Home Harmony** **113**
	What's Fair? Growing and Changing 114
	The Royal WE 117
8	**Finding the Wealth** **119**
	Personal Expression Presenting yourself 122
	Enhancements 124
	Career and Wealth Areas Entrance, Where is the Wealth? 126
	Your Big Goals – What do you want? 129
	Woo-Woo? Weird stuff we can't see… 137
9	**Making the Shift** **139**

Appendix A: More about the Power Position 141
Appendix B: The Expanded Bagua 143
Appendix C: EMF's and You! 147
Appendix D: The PEP QUIZ 153
Author Biography: Kathryn Wilking 157
    More About Kathryn 159
    More About kathrynwilking.com 160
    Happy Clients 162
Epilogue 165

Kathryn Wilking

Forward: Working at Home, or is it *Living at Work*?

The last few years has seen a massive social upheaval, as families strive to find a new work routine and balance, while juggling the chores and realities of the day within their homes. As well, many had to step back from climbing the corporate ladder to face realities of the 'sandwich years'; looking after others older and younger than themselves. And reducing the focus on their jobs can often cultivate more stress!

Setting priorities to meet all the demands of modern day life can be done, cultivating a calm, stress-free, rewarding lifestyle.

So get your space working for you and find the work-life-home-balance by applying the principles of Feng Shui! This book will show you how to find a supportive space to work, set boundaries and be more productive.

My first book, *Practical Feng Shui for the Office; Finding Your Individual Balance in the Workplace,* was published in 2013. It was all about cubicle and corporate lifestyle; setups and in-depth study with The Five Elements of Chinese Medicine.

When Covid came along in 2020, that book lost some of its relevance. It wasn't out of date, but I needed to address the key issues of **working at home**. Through the help of a new publisher, we decided to re-launch parts of the first book and enhance the message with details addressing the vital issues for today: working from home, setting boundaries and dealing with multiple devices all over the house!

The Feng Shui Advantage; Get your Space Working for You!

Kathryn Wilking

Introduction to Feng Shui

The purpose of this book is to take the mystery out of Feng Shui and show you how practical it really is. Feng Shui can give you guidance to become more aware of your surroundings and tools to de-stress your life. For those readers who have not been exposed to Feng Shui, it is more than moving your furniture around and collecting gold coins. I want to present this valuable information in layman's terms and make it simple to understand.

Chi energy is one of our life forces, and it's available for free! It permeates our lives in every way! Just open a door or window and inhale; a deep inhale. Embrace the freshness, that crisp feeling going into your lungs. That life force is chi energy. Your whole house and workspace should include fresh chi energy as best as possible all year 'round.

Whenever I clean up my office, change the sheets or general cleaning, I open a window or the patio door and let the chi energy in to clear, clean and freshen the space. Even a few minutes is beneficial any time of the day.

While traditional Feng Shui is rooted in Buddhist beliefs and relies heavily on a compass, it has evolved through a long journey from India through Tibet and China, at each place absorbing new customs, opportunities and changing needs.

The Feng Shui school I chose to study is the Black Hat Sect (also referred to as Black Tantric Buddhism-BTB). BTB is an amalgamation of many influences. I believe the progressive BTB style is a perfect fit for me and my clients in our modern world.

One of the early Feng Shui concepts expanded upon by the late BTB Grand Master Professor Lin Yun is the Five-Element Theory from Chinese Medicine; part of which forms the basis of this book. When these elements are applied to physical items it is very practical and functional, and then, when applied to the individual, this theory becomes absolutely fascinating! The layers and layers of personality traits within us all start to make sense. This book will take you through the steps in setting up your physical workspace, and then, show you how to understand yourself, family, coworkers and the environment around you.

Feng Shui has many layers. You can shift energy by manipulating things in the environment. And, just when you think you have figured it out, something else emerges. The simple mundane *cures* and *enhancements* mentioned in this book are only the tip of what is possible. They are very practical and as unique as each individual, as they change with the times. Anything that influences you can change the dynamics of your life. Through progress and modernization over thousands of years, the aim of Feng Shui has remained the same: the pursuit of a more comfortable and harmonious place to live and work.

When deciding on where to begin, think in layers. The First Layer is all about function and flow: tangible placement, furniture and scale will all be addressed. The Second Layer is about colours, shapes and images; and their messages that can support you. The Third Layer is more about the things you cannot see: energy, frequencies and a bit of 'woo-woo'.

A Little History

Feng Shui dates back over 4,000 years to a time when the early civilizations in China were seeking burial sites for their ancestors. Their quest to find the perfect resting place for all eternity involved working intimately with the heavens, the earth and the realities of the surrounding terrain. They were also evaluating the lands far and wide in order to find the best place for their families to prosper.

Feng Shui literally translates as 'wind and water'. It is about the energy and movement of things you can see and those you can't. This energy changes from day to day, season to season, year to year. These energy patterns include personal energy in yourself and in your surroundings as well as the vast energy from the cosmos. That energy force mentioned earlier called *chi*, is translated as 'cosmic breath'.

The theory of opposites in the universe, referred to as *yin and yang*, is also part of Feng Shui. Yin is dark, soft and feminine, while yang is light, energetic and masculine. We all have both masculine and feminine attributes in our bodies; again finding the balance. The impact of these influences is apparent in all aspects of our lives. The symbol for yin and yang is similar to two tadpoles intertwined with each other, each possessing a little bit of the other's qualities. Together, they are harmony. Harmony and balance are essential factors in Feng Shui, linking man and the universe.

Today, Feng Shui consultants are not specifically looking for burial grounds, but they still observe the immediate environment and energy flow as influenced by the factors of modern life.

A Feng Shui expert will also look for any changing dynamics of chi energy by taking physics, psychology, architecture and design into consideration in their Feng Shui analyses. This extends from ground, waters and mountains to the actual building design and interior room shapes, angles, colours and placement of furnishings. Within the buildings, they look at how these dynamics work together with the people working and living in the building environment. Other exterior factors that come into consideration in our modern world include adjacent buildings, freeway structures, power lines and of course, electromagnetic frequencies from our computer devices.

Feng Shui never goes out of style, the energy shifts to expose what needs to be done. Enjoy your journey on the road to an organized, productive and balanced lifestyle.

Kathryn Wilking

x

1 Feng Shui Your Cubicle

I'm going to use the word 'cubicle', referring to a small space, as if you were working in a tight, finite office setting. Many families don't have the space for a designated office, and finding the right spot to work can be challenging. If you only have a small table or the corner of the dining room for your workspace, you can *feel* that this isn't a perfect solution. Yet, there is help for you! Any, and all, of these ideas can be applied to help you achieve productivity in your space. YAY!

I have met with so many people in the last few years who apologize for their office or workspace. Apologize? For what? They all appear to be competent, sane people with good jobs, so what is the problem? Well, a lot of them are embarrassed. They don't really like their workspace. The desk is often piled high with projects or papers. I listen to complaints that "This office doesn't really work for me", from many of my clients.

To put you all at ease, you *are working*, right? You are allowed to have papers all over your desk. In fact, having a lot of paper can mean job security these days. The problem is really the flow, the routine and the organizing of the projects. Feng Shui can help you with all of these things.

A Feng Shui workspace should give you a balanced flow of energy so you can accomplish the tasks of the day. The goal is to make your space productive and functional. Achieving that balance means different things for different people. By identifying obstacles and distractions, you can clear the space, and your mind, in order to grow. The balance in your office will be affected by the goals you have for yourself, both for working and in your personal life.

Setting Goals

Some people love a 'vision board'—a poster board or similar setup to focus on your goals, intentions and achievements. They like to *see* things and believe that change will happen. And yet, some goals are hard to pin down as they are in motion; lingering in infancy, ready to change and morph into reality. Think of your desk, or even your entire office or room, as your vision board. Everything you put in there must have a purpose. From there, you can move these goals into reality. The adjustments to your workspace are personal, therefore, don't allow others to interfere.

What you see and what you think will support your life goals.

Reader Challenge

There are a few basic questions you need to ask yourself before setting your goals and intentions for a new start (any time of the year). Write down the goals that you have for the job position you are in right now.

- What do you like about your job?
- What don't you like about your job?
- How do these goals fit with the future of the company?
- Do these goals blend in with your personal goals?

When you have a vision that you can believe in, you are on your way! Your vision does not need to be carved in stone right now. Just turn your head around the corner and view a different perspective on your life.

The Power Position

When you find the right spot to work:

- you automatically become safe, as your back is protected
- you have control as your sight lines are defined
- you are out of the way of distractions

One of the first things to consider in the office is placement of the desk and other furniture. Regardless of whether you have an entire room designated as your office or simply a closet or cubicle, you will need to find the Power Position. (AKA: Command Position) This would be the best spot to place your desk in order to see the whole room and the doorway, yet not be in direct alignment with the doorway.

In your Power Position, you should feel comfortable and relaxed. If you feel good sitting at your desk, it is a good indication that you are on the right track. You may not feel like a success today, but you will enjoy the process of becoming successful in the future. See Figure 1.1.

Things to ponder when setting up your work area in the Power Position:

- If you sit with your back to a door, open space or fire exit, your subconscious could be over-active, wondering what is going on behind your back. Try to get creative with your desk arrangement so you can see the door from your desk.

- If you are unable to find a Power Position that faces the door, consider placing a small mirror (purse-size or convex) discreetly on your desk to face the doorway. This will reflect back to you; if someone's shadow crosses the light behind you, there will be no surprises.

- Avoid sitting with a window behind you. A window is clear and fragile and is not the best way to support your work. Any glare from the window on your PC will also give you a headache. Consider a curtain in a light fabric or a screen divider as a block could help to make you feel more secure.

- A high bookshelf behind you, even fixed to the wall, can give you the feeling of being overwhelmed with too much work to do -hanging over your head. A lower bookshelf or bench behind you could be a better choice.

- Do not place your desk under a beam or under a sloped ceiling. Any configuration that makes you feel anxious, overwhelmed or stifled should be reconsidered.

When making these adjustments, check out more than one configuration. Sit quietly in different directions for a few minutes, or even a full day, to see if this change feels like a Power Position for you.

The Power Position and its complexities refer back to an ancient Chinese model. More details are given in Appendix A.

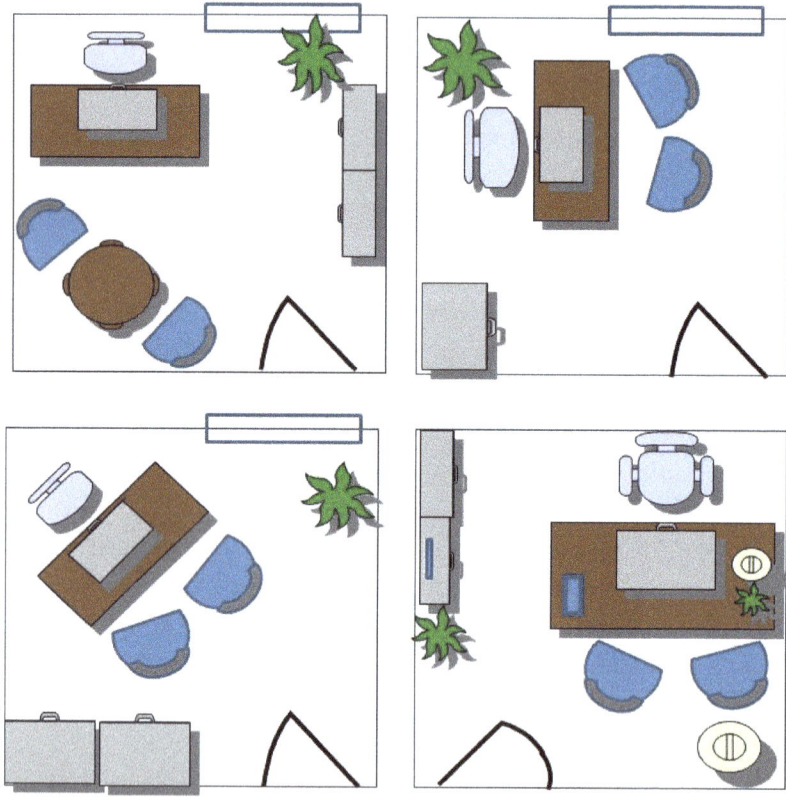

Figure 1.1 These desks are all in the Power Position. The people that work here will have the best range of vision and will avoid being startled or distracted during the day.

Tip: A manager in a group setting should sit in the *most commanding position* to assert authority with his or her team. Anyone who has their workspace too close to the door, they may be constantly interrupted.

Work Stations: The Best Place

Large, modern businesses tend to maximize their employee capacity by setting up little pods, or cubicles grouped together, for their workstations. This could happen if you were required to drop into a flex-hub or checking in to 'the office'. Many workstations are set up for the employee to face a wall or partition. Originally, this was to provide privacy and avoid distractions in an open-concept facility. In reality, you may feel detached; feeling closed off in a closet and unable to see what is going on.

> **FYI:** Not too long ago, an acceptable punishment for a child was to send him/her into a corner, nose to the wall. From there, he/she could not see anyone or find out what was going on. Do you ever feel punished or out of touch in a small space facing a wall?

Take these factors into consideration when evaluating your total workspace from a Feng Shui perspective:

- If your workspace faces another person without a divider, this will only work if you are sharing the same project. You may be more productive by facing *away* one-quarter-turn to allow for personal space.

- If you are stationed at the end of a long hallway, you'll have other concerns. Long hallways can become stagnant; without enough fresh air reaching the desk; or the opposite, with full-force energy streaming toward you.

- Indoor air quality is another necessity. Also check for good lighting, sounds, odours, heating and A/C. Make sure your chosen space is a comfortable zone for you to work.

- Pay attention to vacant areas, junk rooms or dead space. These areas can collect clutter and become stagnant. You could bring in some bright objects or plants to balance out inactive space.

- Check out the traffic flow in the room. Are you situated near the bathroom door, lunch room or break room? All this additional traffic can interrupt you from being productive. (See figure 1.2.)

- Pay attention to your view when you enter a room or look up from your desk. If the view is split—one eye focused on long distance and the other near. Your brain needs to process *every time* you look up. This very simple issue could be the main thing that is sabotaging the quality of your work.

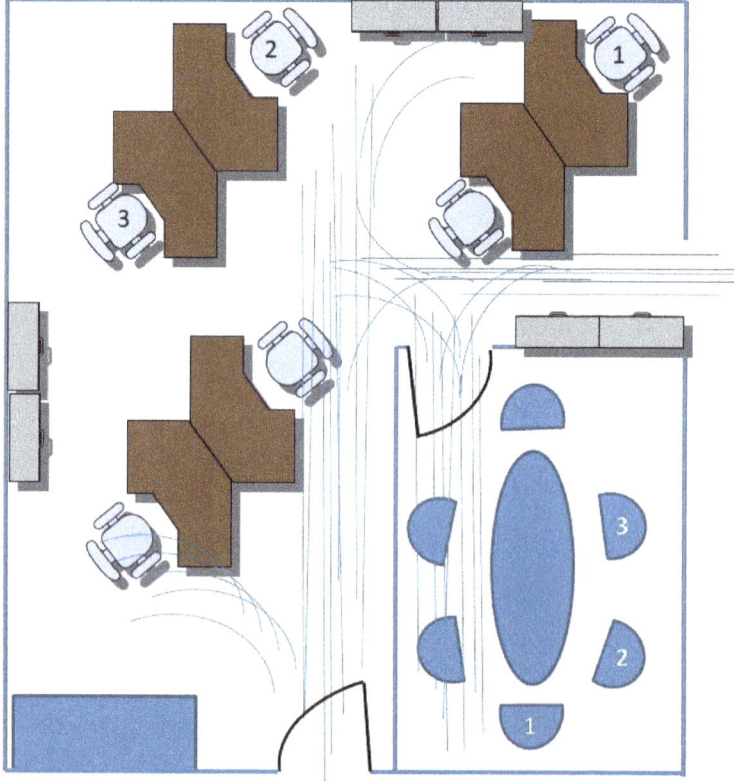

Figure 1.2 Be aware of how the energy and traffic flows through the office. Disruptive energy comes in from elevators, lunch room and other traffic. Best places to sit: Seats 1,2 or 3 as shown in both the closed office and in open concept. A few well placed room-dividers could make this space more productive.

- Electromagnetic fields (EMFs) are of concern in modern homes and offices. With unlimited wireless pulses from our devices (and everyone else's), many people can become fatigued from the nonstop pulsing on our brains and bodies. Be aware of these EMFs. Every wireless phone, computer, printer, mouse and more all carry their own vibration. Research on this topic is still on going. Be aware of your environment. For further reading on this subject, check out Appendix C.

- Look for poison arrows. A poison arrow is a perceived line drawn from a corner or sharp edge that points directly at you. Arrows can also show up in many way aiming at your front or your back. (See figure 1.3.)

Is there a best place for your desk? Absolutely! In an ideal world, you could choose the perfect spot for yourself. Choosing the 'best spot' to work can be a challenge in tight quarters or limited choices, you may need to get a little creative.

You need to feel comfortable with the direction you are facing for the space to work. If you can find a spot where you can be happy, have some natural light, enjoy a little privacy and still be aware what is going on, you will be set up for success!

This may appear to be a lot of trivial details to deal with at the office. I understand. And, not everyone is sensitive to all of these issues. If you are set up and 'okay' working under a large beam (for example) that is just fine. And yet, if you are unhappy, unproductive and feeling bogged down most days, you might want to try moving your desk.

Do you still feel punished or unappreciated working in a cramped space? Isolated and alone? There's more creative options for you in Chapter 7.

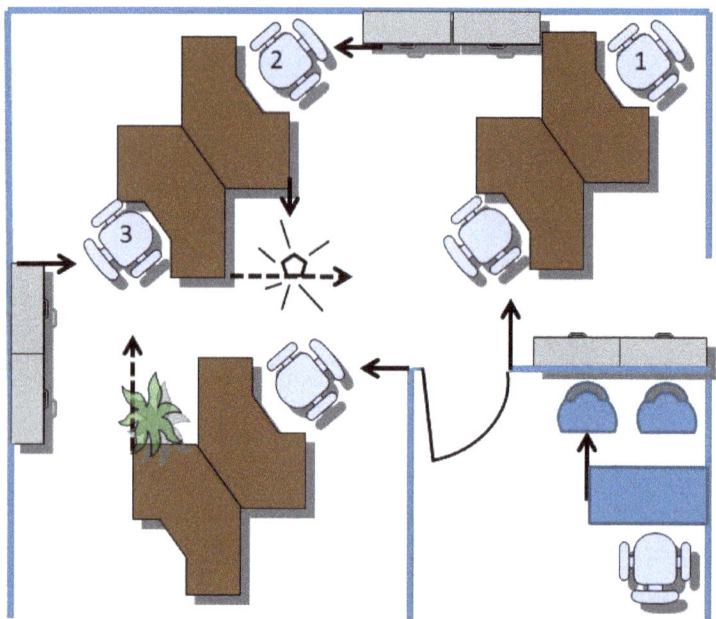

Figure 1.3 Poison arrows are the result of poor alignment in the office layout. Watch for any sharp edge pointing towards you from any direction: a doorway, desk corner, cabinet, pillar or any piece of furniture. Whether you are seated at your home or workspace, watch for these annoyances; large or small.
 To 'cure' a poison arrow, either rearrange your chair or utilize a plant, lamp, or a room divider to soften the sharp edge. Also, a well-placed wind chime or a crystal can diffuse the arrow.

If poison arrows are not bothersome to you, be aware of any changes in your workspace. Have another look in a few weeks, as these distractions can affect your peak performance, and induce anxiety.

* Seats #2 and #3 have filing cabinets immediately at their backs.

The Feng Shui Advantage

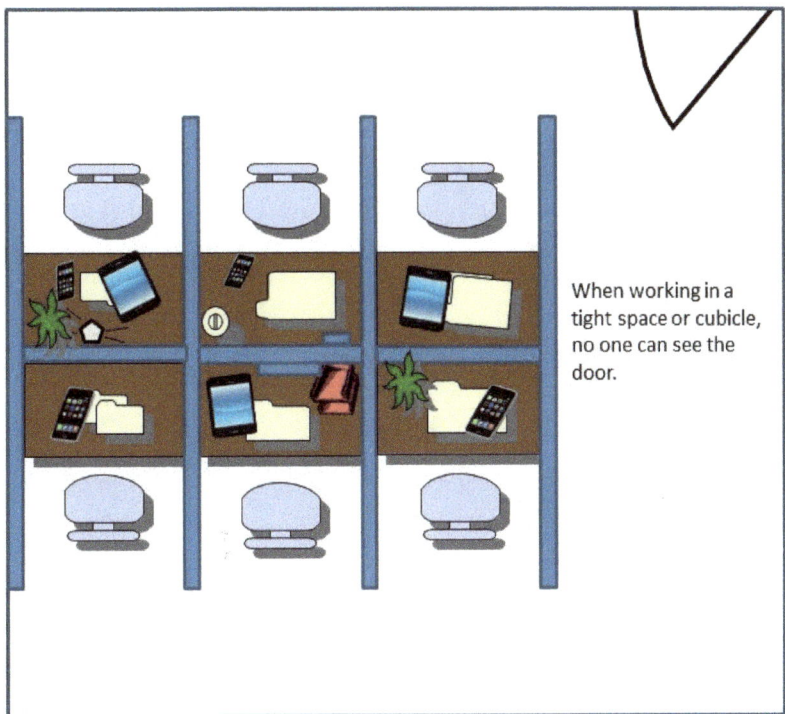

When working in a tight space or cubicle, no one can see the door.

Figure 1.4 Trying to be productive in a tight space can become stressful without the ability to move about and see what's going on.
Without a barrier, sitting directly across from anybody who is bothersome, can also be stressful. Place a quality, crystal paperweight or plant on the space between the two positions and create a better atmosphere.

Not sure how to set up your space? Creative thinking! Be sure to set up shared space to work for all parties involved. Arrange for both privacy and communication.

The Feng Shui Advantage

A couch is a great spot for a break, and yet, setting up a table and chair will boost productivity.

Choosing Your Desk and Chair

A solid desk is a powerful tool. You'll want to choose a desk that is strong and supportive. Poor choices include any desk that is wobbly, lacking support, propped up or made of glass.

- If your desk is sturdy, it will give you support.
- If your desk is large, you will feel confident and competent to move with positive energy in your endeavours.
- If your desk was previously owned by a successful individual who you respect, good feelings will bring you good benefits.
- If your desk is too small and tight, you may be undermining your goals and achievements.

Give the same attention in choosing your chair as you have given to selecting your desk. A chair with armrests will provide you with strength and securities, helping you stay strong in the Power Position. Check for smooth rotation of the wheels and height adjustments to find a proper fit.

Paper and Desk Clutter

A cluttered desk can be the most unproductive desk. I know, we all get busy. It is common to see a desk cluttered with projects in progress and things to file all mixed up together.

The piles with projects *in progress* actually have good energy! It is okay to have them out on the desk. They represent job security: a task, fulfillment, a puzzle, the work order, creativity and money! The rewards for a job well done!

It is the unfinished projects that gather dust, deplete energy on the desk and slow down the motivation necessary to finish the task. These are the items that need to get moved *off the desk first* and into another area: file box, file folder, trash or passed off to someone who will take care of it.

Take time to sort out the small stuff. Yes, this is important. Set a time to deal with personal issues, pay bills and move things away from your immediate working space. Some people sort their work flow left-to-right, or right-to-left; what ever works for you. Some people *need to see* ALL the projects in view; if so, can you put them into some order? Other people need to tuck everything away except for the *one thing* they are working on, which can lead to losing things: out-of-sight = out-of-mind.

You already know what is working for you, or not. More about Clutter Habit Clues to help manage your stuff is in Chapter 5, relating these habits to your personality.

Getting organized may need to be regularly scheduled. Do not jeopardize your efficiency by procrastinating about what to do with the files on your desk. Dead files are ... dead files.

Here's a checklist to consider:

- Clean, clean, clean!
- Try to keep the desk free of clutter directly in front of where you sit. This actually encourages you to sit at your desk. (There will be room to do this.)

- If you are working on a table or sharing space, place a placemat or boundaries to designate your prime work area. This can help focus your attention.
- When you are finished with a file, move it off to the side to give your complete attention to the next task.
- Anything that is dead, dying, stale, forgotten or redundant should be removed. All of these items have potential to block your creativity and productivity.
- There is no need to purchase more and more filing cabinets to store things. Sort through the files you have and purge what you don't need; you'll open up more storage for current clients and projects.

As soon as you get the paper clutter sorted out, you'll be able to find ways to see things differently. Don't allow anyone else to help clear your desk. This is your space.

Tip: While you are rearranging your desk, be sure to clear out the drawers too. Get into the corners and little boxes full of things. When you are finished, you'll notice a huge weight has been lifted from your shoulders.

The Meeting: Where Do I Need to Sit?

Outside of your cubicle, common areas have their own Feng Shui considerations. When heading into meeting rooms, waiting areas in reception or even a restaurant, arriving early always gives you the advantage. Choose a seat where you can see the entire room and the door, so there will be no surprises.

The chairman or manager running the meeting usually sits at the head of the meeting table. Choose to sit on one side of the speaker or the other, while still being able to see the door. All eyes will be on the presentation and therefore you will be seen as important too. On the opposite end of the table, the person closest to the door may be distracted with interruptions. This individual could be the one designated to gather forgotten supplies, take messages, check the lights and so on.

Plan ahead and choose your seat. When you find the spot where you feel grounded, focused and productive, you will be in the best position for success.

Check out meeting rooms and their patterns on Fig 1.5.

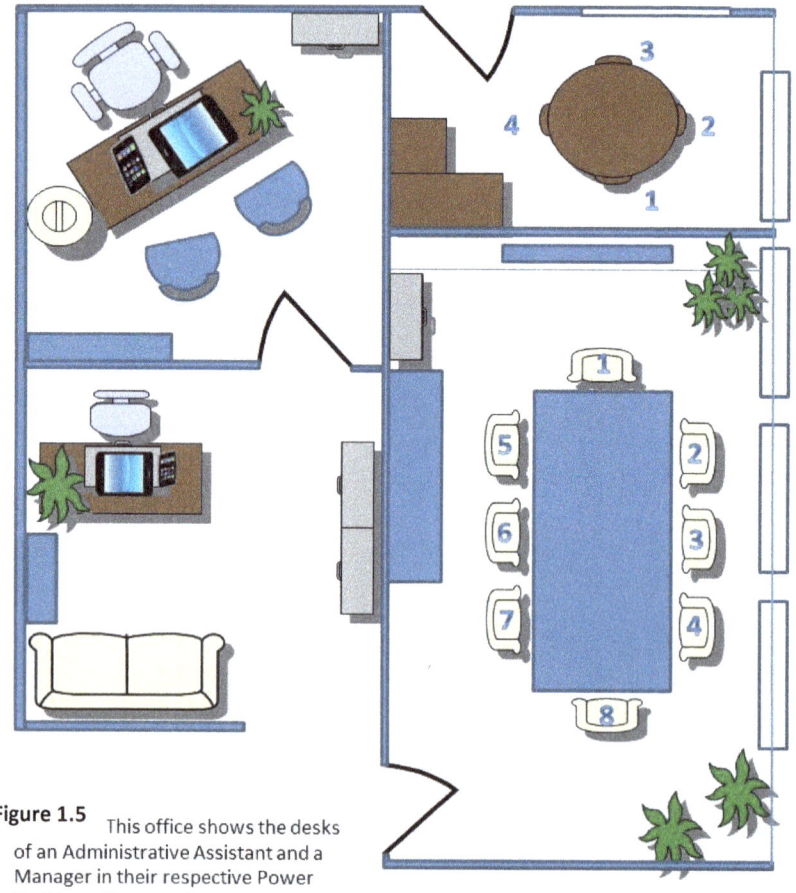

Figure 1.5 This office shows the desks of an Administrative Assistant and a Manager in their respective Power Positions. The Meeting Room and Break Room show the best places to sit (starting with 1) in order to see the doorway and still be in charge of their sight line.

ZOOM Etiquette

Video conferencing is now high on the list of things you *need to master* for business and personal use! Zoom, Skype and Facetime, usage went UP 2000% in the first few months' of Covid in 2020. WOW!

Once reserved for the sole purpose of external-department conference calls, we now use this for distance learning, visiting relatives, and so much more! Some things, such as internet communications, have changed history forever.

We are not going back, so let's talk about this.

I used video conferencing to check on my aging father long before Covid. It was great that we could set up a call a few times a week to chat. I know he really looked forwards to these chats. I could hear and *see* if he was well as we chatted about the day.

One of the reasons I'm writing about this subject was prompted by a client's comment and an actual screen shot in a situation early in Covid-days. There was a guy, fresh out of the shower who signed into a webinar and proceeded to lotion-up and get dressed in front of the camera! Yes, in the BUFF! And, it was shared all over the internet! YIKES!

> **Your Zoom presence is the modern-day business card!**
> Use this tool wisely! Since many of us are now working almost exclusively from home, we need to reframe this screen space as an extension of our business.
>
> This is where you meet with clients, coworkers, sell your products and establish a positive and personable reputation. Your image reveals a story to people on the other end: what is going around in your surroundings.

If you are on a video call and then take a phone call no one gets your full attention.

I've seen politicians preach from their kitchen, meetings in living rooms, and a guy giving a presentation *as his wife walked by with a load of laundry*! Ouch! Let's pay attention and be professional.

Camera on face:

Which ever device you are using, please take the time to *check* what others are seeing.

The camera should be equal to or slightly above your eyes.

- If the lens is *too low*, you'll reveal too much of the ceiling.
- A tiny head *cut off* at the jaw does nothing to boost your presence; you run the risk of looking lost and unprofessional. Just raise the lens on your device a few inches higher.
- If your camera is placed *very low* on a coffee table, the viewer gets a view up-your-nose, or perhaps a crotch-shot!
- People want to see your face, therefore, turn on the lights!
- Be present. Center yourself from shoulders or waist up, so people can see and hear you properly.

Camera on background:

Choosing a background can also set a tone/mood for the call. Standing in front of a brick wall could stifle creative conversation and connection, while a plain wall can be 'warmed' up with a plant or bookshelf (neatness counts).

For a casual one-on-one chat, you may feel comfortable to share the kitchen as you enjoy a coffee. That's okay.

Choosing the 'best-place' to sit and participate on a client call could be a puzzle, but take a look around and plan ahead for these video calls. A full webinar meeting may require you to 'show up' as the professional that you are. Chapter 1 of this book can review the best position for you.

If you are talking on video with *paying clients* and virtually inviting them into your home, let's expand on this plan. Think about what is behind you:

- Others don't want to see posters of your 'GOALS FOR THE YEAR'. Example: the sailboat you are saving up to buy or your sales goals for the year. These goals are for you.
- Hide your 'quirks' as they could offend others regarding hobbies, habits, religious items or sports teams.
- A background revealing an open closet door can certainly peek curiosity. If your services are to be 'credible, organized and helpful' to a client, a crowded mess in the background could alter their opinion of you.

SO, you don't have a designated area for a video? This is where we can get creative!

Find a space that will give you enough room to set up a computer and chair. Check your background.

Some of my clients use a room divider of sorts or sheer curtains strung across the room. Others hang a large oil painting/print (no glare) that works with their branding décor. Utilize calm colours and be aware of any sensitivities mentioned above.

Alternatively, most video platforms allow you to 'blur' the background. Another option: consider *uploading your own image* of an imaginary office, meeting rooms, backyard or vacation shot. It's important to represent yourself properly. Make appropriated choices that relates to your business or lifestyle.

Reveal only whatever seems appropriate. Please take the time to sort this out today.

When to turn off - Use good manners

- Please, turn AUDIO and VIDEO camera off until to are ready to begin. Finish eating, chewing and coughing. Pay attention!
- If you have to leave, click off both your AUDIO AND VIDEO. When leaving a chair empty, it can be insulting to the presenter and others.
- Sneezing and coughing: Can you do this quietly? Please *mute* yourself!

I know many of these things give you a chuckle, and we are only human. And yet, this does happen; **someone will see the replay!**

Using Zoom, Skype and the like to stay connected can help make more connections and is now so essential for us to thrive. Using these video tools, as tools, can help form a foundation in business for what lies ahead. **Use this tool wisely.**

At the Coffee Shop

Being stuck or cramped up at home is no fun. A visit to the local Coffee Shop or Library can provide a much needed break and hopefully you can find a stimulating environment.

More and more coffee shops are allowing work/study patrons, promoting they have full internet service. Yet, there is more to consider. When working in an alternative location, you'll still need to be in the 'best seat' in order to be in the power position and be productive away from home.

You've probably already figured out that everyone's first choice is to grab a booth; but you may not know why!

First choice, a booth creates protective space. You'll be free from anyone walking behind you, knocking your elbow or exiting from kitchen or bathroom access.

Second choice, select a seat next to a wall. Again, this allows for some protection and privacy, but you may not have control over noise or distractions.

Third choice, tables in the middle of the room. This is where you'll be interrupted, bumped, and experience excess noise. You'll probably leave early; plan alternative locations.
You need to be aware of what goes on in a public space; be sure to see the enter/exit doors and know when to leave. Similar habits for your office, remember these guidelines when choosing a seat:

- Your back need to be protected – no need to get your subconscious in high-alert; stay calm.
- Recognize the supports around you: a wall or solid boundaries. Check for a safe Wi-Fi connection, good lighting and horizontal space to spread out.

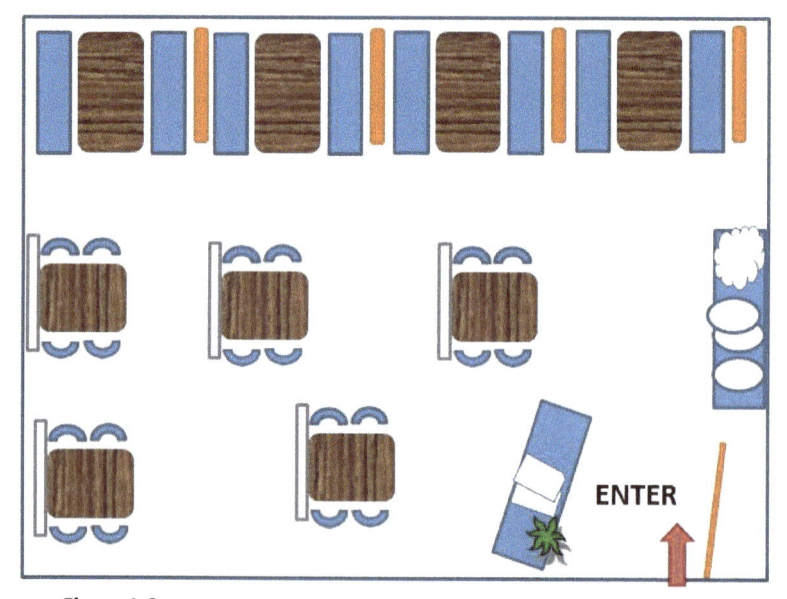

Figure 1.6

Joe's Cafe: Have you ever noticed that in any sit-down eatery, the first places to get taken are the booths?
After they are gone, everyone sits around the edges.
And then, what's left are the middle seats.
Most people *instinctively* know to keep their back protected.
No one enjoys kitchen noise or people moving behind them.

When using other people's space, or in public spaces, please act respectfully. Clean up your mess, say thank you and make a reasonable purchase from the establishment. If too many others abuse this courteous of sharing space, the option would be to discontinue people working in the café.

Set an example for others.

Kathryn Wilking

2 Inside the Home
Working from Home

First of all, Bless the Mess! Making room for living and working in the home is a 24/7 commitment. Your space will not be meticulously cleaned up every day.

We are going to focus this chapter on sharing spaces. When we are space-sharing in the home, we need to set boundaries in order to be productive while working or studying.

How does someone go about 'finding a balance'? A busy house translates to continuous maintenance and chores that need to be done: laundry, dishes, shopping for food, menu planning, garbage, recycling, cleaning floors, bathrooms and, so much more.

Trying to get-it-all-done, or even stay-on-top-of-it can be a marathon. Here's a few things I did to take the pressure off me.

When my boys got old enough, they were required to help out with chores. And then, when they need spending money, they negotiated what each chore was worth! They required spending money and I needed the carpets vacuumed! Win-win!

I also decided to only cook 3 days a week. Yep, a real time saver! I cooked a huge meal on Sundays, Tuesdays and Thursday's. I cooked enough for (hopefully) leftovers on the off days and assumed the teens had enough culinary skills to get though the gaps. On the weekends, we had options; choosing to eat-out or take-away.

> There was a poem on my Mother-in-Law's kitchen that reminded us all to be grateful:
>
> *Thank God for dirty dishes*
> *As they have tale to tell.*
> *By this stack of evidence*
> *We are eating rather well.*

Plan for days to deal with the small-stuff; we need those days to organize and set up for success! When you find yourself completing 'all the little, boring things in life', you can be sure, the rest of the week is going to be *just fine.* Taking the time for the small things in life, will set you up for success for the rest of the week!

Regarding Feng Shui, it's easy to say: "Surround yourself with the things you LOVE and everything will fall into place." But it's more than that. Finding a *system* that works will help you to sleep better, cultivate solid relationships, thrive in your work and make sound decisions for the future.

Does this translate to less stress? You bet!

Cultivating the Flow

The first step is to figure out function and flow for each person in the house. Let's take a step back and look at the dynamics of the family; the more people in the home requires more compromising. The odds of having extra bedrooms or private space for everyone are pretty small except for a small percentage of the population.

A functioning family, just like your job setting, requires that everyone is seen and heard.

Working in Common Areas

The global pandemic really changed the modern family lifestyle, as there is now a greater demand to fill our homes with multiple devices for everyone. Technology is progressing very quickly. And, if you try to ignore this growing need to ingest every video, post and newsfeed available, you will be left behind.

Trying to concentrate and work on separate projects in common areas can be a bit tricky. Creating privacy can be a bit delicate. Regardless of how many people, everyone needs a chair and a work station.

How much space does each person need? How do we find more space?

First, let's utilize the horizontal surfaces: kitchen island, dining room table, pop up coffee table, utility table, kiddy desk.

Whatever that space is, define how MUCH space each person needs:

- Is this space to be used primarily for writing essays, homework on line, playing games? I.e. taking up a minimum amount of space.
- Does this space require 'additional space' to house text books, reference materials or other? I.e. more space than above.
- Can this space be cleared easily for multi-purpose use? ie: meals, class projects, groceries?

The answers to these questions will guide you as to who needs how much space. Compromise is good, but not always fair. And remember, these requirements could change every few months!

Everyone needs space boundaries in order to establish a routine.

- Be respectful. Use noise cancelling headphones or ear buds to avoid distractions.
- Younger school-aged kids should NOT be positioned 'looking at each other' (!)
- Younger school-aged kids may need an adult present.
- Older kids and young adults who can self-monitor themselves should need less supervision; allowing them to work independently.
- Schedule Audio calls or ZOOM when less disruptive to others. Perhaps another room for calls is needed.
- All adult-aged kids in the home require a designated space for themselves, not a shared table.
- Don't expect anyone to sit and work for the whole day. Book 'coffee breaks', walks outside or other rewards to balance out sedentary sitting. Also, plan to give your eyes a break from the screen.

Which time of the day could be your best productive time with the least amount of distractions? What I'm finding is that many working moms are trying to teach/supervise their kids, as well as, be productive in their own work.

Set boundaries. Could talking and asking questions wait until lunch hour or after a certain time?

Check out some new furniture options for pop-up coffee tables and TV trays. If you find yourself sharing a corner of the dining room table, whether it be for a spouse or children, set out boundaries for all parties. Designate a space that represents 'Time for Work-Study';

AKA: –Do not disturb and DO NOT touch my stuff.

You don't need to be chained to one primary work area. If you can work part of the time in one area and then another area for another 'shift', it won't feel like you are living in one room for 24 hrs a day. For many of us, shorter sprints of work/study may be more productive if working in a cramped space.

Tip: Reminder to set up rules about time management and what you plan to achieve each shift on the computer. You all know how easy it is to blink and loose a few hours of productivity!

If your set-up is under the stairs or tucked into a closet, this position takes away your sight lines. You'll be missing details. Place a mirror in this space to help see what is happening behind you.

Often, these temporary decisions end up being permanent. Spending large amounts of time without natural light, proper heating, or other interaction could be unproductive. Working in a not-so-great-area may require more breaks because your unconscious can *feel* unrest and anxiety. Therefore, plan regular breaks, and then, get back to your tasks.

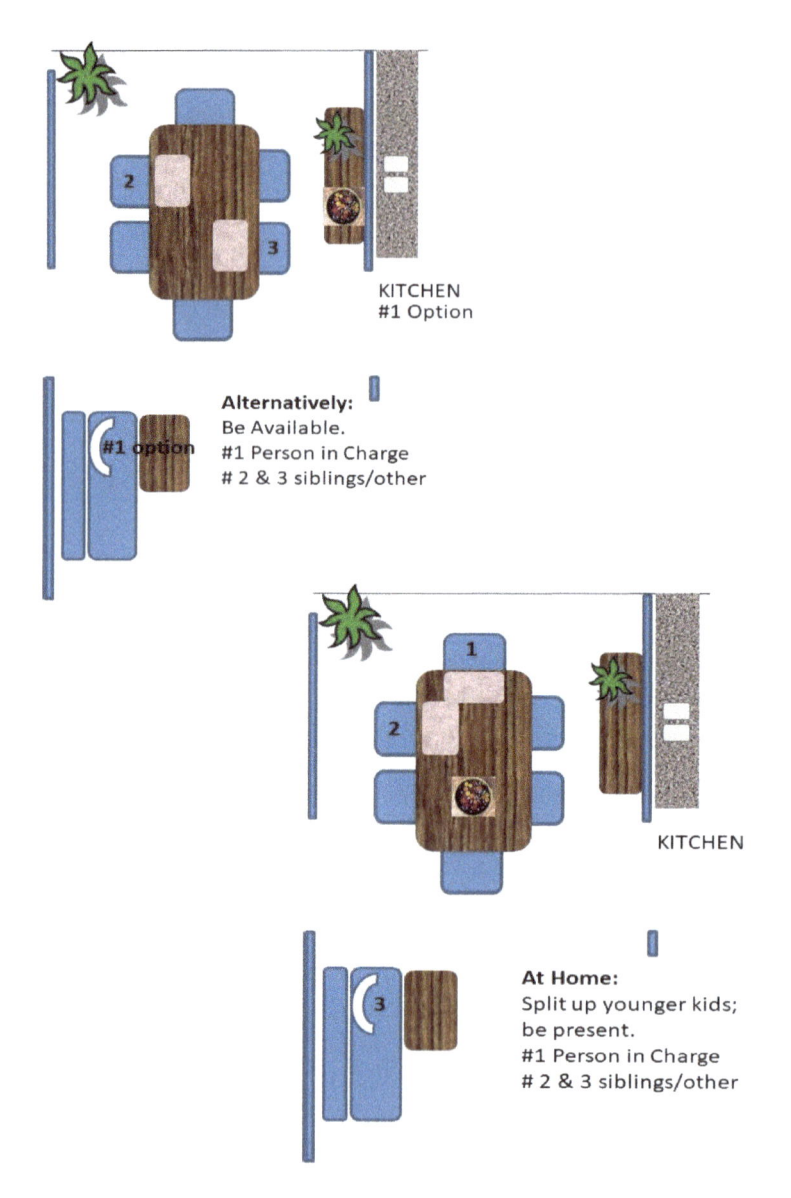

Figures 2.1 A&B Setups for Common Areas

The Person-In-Charge is shown in two different supervisory positions, depending on the needs and ages of everyone involved.

This issue of using space to do 'double duty' can be tricky; most 'cures' are very specific to each person's needs. However, many people manage to work in spaces that are 'not the best' situations: in closets, under the stairs, downstairs, in a garage and so on. Be aware that *if* the spot is not ideal, you can still make adjustments to your space to make it work better for you.

Working in a room that is assigned for sleeping is not the most productive choice. Bedrooms are supposed to be yin-energy; quiet, restful and restorative. Office situations require more yang-energy for motivation, taking initiative and meeting goals. If you add in distractions of a computer and Wi-Fi into your bedroom, this energy will disrupt your sleep. Therefore, you have conflicting purposes – sleep or work?

Yin and yang energy can be confusing. Do you 'dream' about work? Or, are you napping in the middle of the day? Sharing these energies can be distracting.

I've seen many work stations set up in primary bedrooms; sharing this space usually doesn't work. In this case the energy displaced here is equal to having a spin bike in the bedroom! Different energies don't mix easily. **A primary bedroom should not be a flex room.**

Ideally, you do not want any phones or Wi-Fi in your bedroom as they are proven to disrupt sleep patterns. If you do not have the space for a room divider, I would suggest keeping as many of your 'work materials' (files, reference materials, project work) outside of the bedroom.

Here are a few corrections that you can put into place right away:

- Arrange your desk to be 'in the power position' if possible.
- For a visual distraction: Place a room-divider between you and the bed or doorway.
- To cultivate energy: Place a floor lamp/flowers/or lively image in this area.
- Minimize the Wi-Fi exposure: Can you connect your computer directly to a modem? Can you move the printer and other gadgets to another room?

Tip: I usually place a colourful table cloth on my desk, and then, change it up with the seasons. You can also use a favorite scarf or placemat to claim your space. Have fun with this!

Tip: In one client's home, I utilized an ironing board to act as a desk. She was happy to work with a stand-up desk in short bursts and it kept all her stuff off the kitchen table!

Tip: It's okay to move over to the couch or the kitchen when you are working on lighter tasks. This action signals a break from 'task-working' when you change environments.

Regardless where you end up sitting: Protect your boundaries and productive working hours. *Review the Power Position in Chapter One.

Supportive Décor

Visual decoration can influence your mood and motivation. Choose all your pictures, artwork and items carefully so that they actually reflect your goals and intentions.

The colours, shapes and images chosen to decorate your space can be either supportive or they can sabotage your efforts.

Refer back to yin and yang; as they are opposites in the universe, you need to be aware of their impact. Each and every decision you make will have a different impact; make sure these decisions support and inspire you.

Consciously uplift your spirit towards your goals and successes, regardless of whether you have a private office or shared space.

The goal is to surround yourself with the things you love and will support you! What do you need for décor in your type of work? A sales office may need something flashy and aggressive; while a space that specializes in healing work would prefer something calm.

If there is an abundance of sports teams and super hero images display all around the room, these pictures could distract from necessary, productive work.

For each adjustment, or 'cure', you need to select each item specifically for your personal requirements for the space. A slower, yin workstyle could benefit by utilizing softer items and textiles: drapery, chair cushions and placemats. Yin energy embraces softer colours when requiring a slower pace; contemplating a solution, editing a book or spiritual practise.

If you need to stay energized, witty and inspired, you'll need yang energy. Yang energy is cultivated by utilizing hard surfaces, sharp, shiny or reflective items in your environment. This stimulation can keep you motivated through your work day.

A few notes for inspiration:

- a large heavy object or sculpture can help you be grounded into a project.
- Maybe you like to travel. A map of the world could be related to your travel goals, a measurement of success, or it could be a total distraction, leading you to envision all the places in the world you could never possibly visit.
- Moving or rushing water on a poster can represent a busy, multitasking space or an endless outpouring of energy; exhilarating for some, very exhausting for others.
- Anxiety can be balanced with artwork. Displaying a tranquil lake or larger body of water can promote a calmer foundation for planning projects and security to the group.

Whatever you choose for the decor, it should be fabulous! Everything must inspire you and represent the goals and intentions you have set out. Be sure to participate if others are choosing furnishings for a shared or common area.

As you grow and move through life, you may be drawn to different supportive décor. Just swap things out.

Tip: Are you are ready to go shopping? You *know* which colours and images inspire you. Let them start working for you.

Reader Challenge

Take a few minutes to identify the distractions in your workspace. *Does this office inspire me to be productive every day?* The longer you've been working in the space, the harder it is to identify those distractions. It's probably time to shift things!

If you aren't inspired by one or more of your furnishings, it is time to replace them with something that works for you. I personally find the best reset happens after totally clearing out the space, and repainting. Then, bring back only the things that support you the best. Open yourself and your space to experience new horizons and growth.

Real Case Study: I've worked with a man, Ken, whose desk was 'sharing space' with a drum set, luggage and power tools! He told me he hardly sat in that room. I was actually called to the house because of a home invasion, and then, he asked me to 'look into his 'office'.

I was in there for all of 5 minutes and left him with a list: Clean up the mess, sell the drum set, paint the walls a lighter colour and of course, turn your desk to be in the Power Position. (Refer to Chapter One). Ken asked, "Can't you see that my desk has a tall hutch all around it, how do I do that?" I suggested he *could* take off the hutch parts, turn the desk, and then, try it out for a bit – no need to buy a new desk.

He called me in amazement a week later after he finished painting. He'd taken his desk apart, sold the drum set and was delighted that his home office was *'so much bigger'.*

Real Case Study: A lovely lady, Siri, didn't know how to work at home and still watch her toddler. We chose the family room area as it had more space to work with and was on the ground floor. We turned the desk and chair into the Power Position so she could have natural light and see all around the room and into the kitchen. She had room for everything she needed for the work day on the ground floor; there was no reason to unplug and walk her devices about the house.

The best part: I set up a work station in the corner of the Family Room for her toddler. I placed a little stool and bench next to her desk so the child could 'visit' and play quietly with a toy or truck. When the child gets a bit older, he can use this space to draw or color pictures while mom works. In addition, the mom managed to arrange shared childcare a few hours a week; so she did get intermittent breaks. The result: part-time work with a child in the house can be done.

Real Case Study: One client was so depressed when she phoned me. Nothing was going right in her home and business! The couple was married only a year ago and the woman had set up a desk to work in the master bedroom. I went to see her large 4-bedroom home.

One bedroom was chockfull of wedding gifts still in the boxes! Another was set up for the mother-in-law to visit, and then, another bedroom was designated to her shrine and Buddha. The house was stuffed! Her problem was obvious to me- too much furniture and too many bulk-buying items.

Gently, for the greater good, I gave her permission to move the working desk into the spiritual room with Buddha. Within a week, her life changed! She still had a lot of work to do to organize the house, yet, she was happier, confident, connecting better with her husband and looking forwards to having a solid marriage once again.

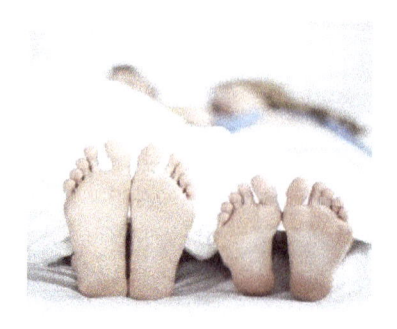

Don't let your work come between you!

3   The Tool Box

The Bagua Grid

When you have your desk in the Power Position and a few accessories selected, we can add another tool to help you focus on your objective: the bagua grid. The bagua grid hosts **The Nine Areas of Life**. By applying the principles of the bagua to your space, you can get that space working for you.

When I first heard about these 'Nine Areas of Life', I just thought "Really? I can't do this! I'm a working mom and my life is between work, sleep and groceries! *NINE* areas? Are you nuts!"

It was then explained to me that by focusing on only 2-3 areas that needed the most help, I would also see transformation in other areas due to the ripple effect of the energy.

You'll notice on the next page the bagua grid is divided into Nine Areas of Life. (fig. 3.1)
- The three areas closest to the door are the areas that regularly interact with the outside world.
- The three areas in the back represent private or personal spaces.
- And, the three areas in the middle are closest to your heart and emotions.

The BTB bagua is a layout or grid that is used to divide any area into nine sub-areas.

The Bagua

WEALTH AND ABUNDANCE Wood Element	FAME AND REPUTATION Fire Element	RELATIONSHIPS AND PARTNERSHIPS Earth Element
FAMILY Wood Element	HEALTH AND VITALITY Earth Element	CHILDREN AND CREATIVITY Metal Element
KNOWLEDGE AND WISDOM Earth Element	CAREER AND LIFEPATH Water Element	HELPFUL PEOPLE AND TRAVEL Metal Element

doorway

Fig. 3.1 Use this Simple Bagua Grid to find the auspicious areas of your home or office.

The Bagua Grid is flexible for many areas:

Line up the Bagua Grid with the red line at the entrance to your entire house, an individual room or smaller items, such as your desk or dresser.

The idea is to identify and reinforce those areas where needed. Each *gua* relates to a particular life area. Each life area is defined with its own element, colour, shape, number, season and more. I cannot tell you specifically what you need in each area, as each area should be personally accented by *you*, with things that are important to *you*!

This bagua is sometimes viewed as an *energy map*—a map of auspicious fortunes of the Nine Areas of Life:

1. Family
2. Wealth and abundance
3. Fame
4. Relationships
5. Children and creativity
6. Helpful people and travel
7. Careers
8. Knowledge and self-cultivation
9. Health

The bagua has infinite applications, and we can only address a few in this book. Although it is often shown as an octagon, I'll be representing the bagua in the form of a grid for ease of use in your floorplan.

The bagua can be stretched and layered for multi purposes. Feng Shui consultants will superimpose the bagua onto just about anything: rooms, buildings and building lots, a floor plan of a house or office, a bookcase, a piece of furniture and more.

A practitioner can use this tool to interpret what is going on in a person's life and recommend cures or enhancements for the area. The application is fairly simple. If a person wants to improve their finances, he/she may want to enhance the Wealth Area of both the workspace and home, as well, choose to enhance the Fame and Career Areas as well.

How to place the bagua for your desk or a specific object:

Line the bottom edge of the grid to the edge of the desk where you sit. Regardless of what shape or size your desk is, divide your desk into nine areas—three equal parts horizontally and vertically. Make a note as to where your strongest and weakest areas are located and what is in these areas.

> The bagua is sometimes pronounced as pa-gua or bakua. The word *gua* translates to 'area' or 'space'. There are other sects that have different interpretations of the bagua not discussed in this book. Appendix B has further insights with the Expanded Bagua.

When placed over a larger area, your entire work area or floor of the building, the bagua is lined up the same: Orient the bottom line with the doorway or entrance to the area. Defining the entrance is very important. This area is extremely auspicious, as it is often described as the 'mouth of chi.' If your entrance to any space is blocked or cluttered, chances are the chi energy is not able to fully circulate in that space.

Tip: When people describe their problems or issues as indecision, procrastination or lack of fulfillment, an easy cure is to clear the entrance area. Allow opportunities to come inside.

The Feng Shui Advantage

Figure 3.2 A simple Bagua placed on a desk shows the positions of your Nine Life Areas. In order for you to work on your goals, reinforce these life areas with specific enhancements relevant to you.
I.e. place Wealth goals in the far left, Fame and Recognition items in the center, and Relationship goals in the far right corner.

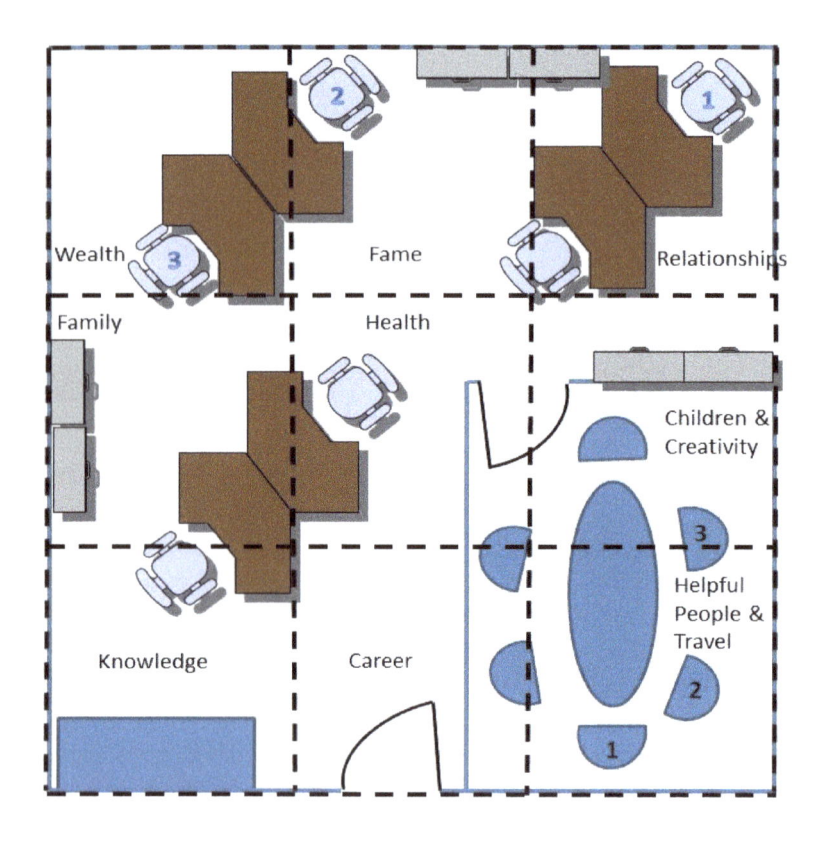

Figure 3.3 This Bagua is applied to a small group office. Each area is available for enhancements, depending on the goals or intentions set by the shared office.

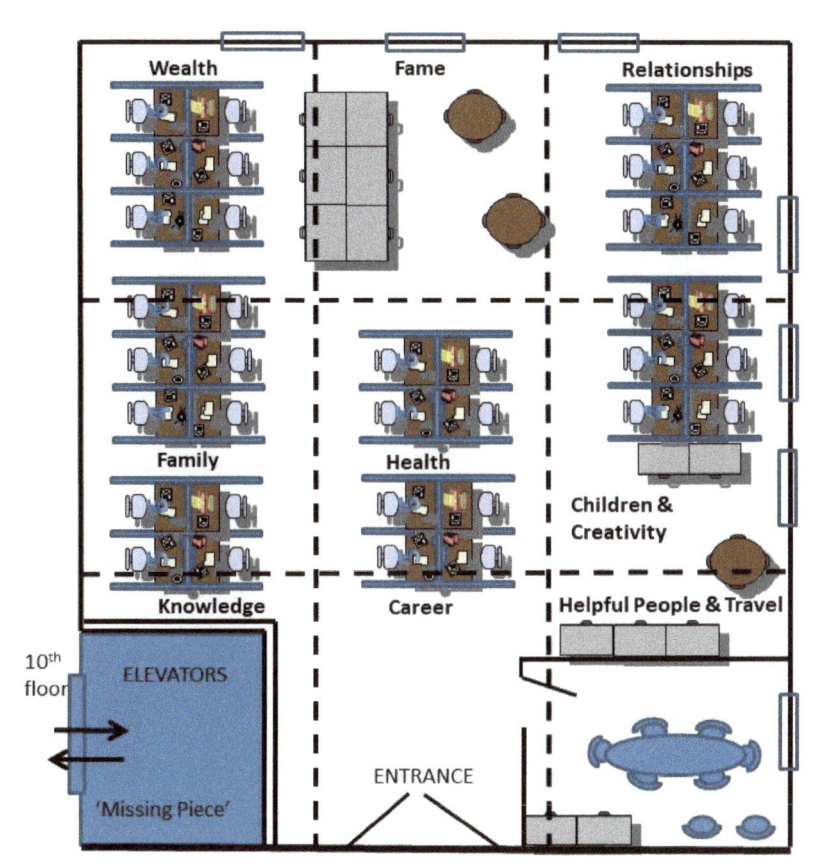

Figure 3.4 This Bagua is applied to an entire office floor. All life areas could be 'enhanced' in order to support business and personal goals.
There are two major issues with this office space: The Career Area in the entrance is not grounded as it is totally void of reinforcements. Also, this floor is missing a large piece of the Knowledge Area, where the elevators are located. Refer to Appendix B regarding 'missing pieces'.

The Five Elements

We use the Five-Element Theory in Chinese Medicine to relate *tangible objects* in your space, such as your desk and decor, to the different elements. Each element is assigned auspicious characteristics relating to colour, shapes and images. To get you started thinking in these terms, here are the elements and a few examples of what they represent:

1. Wood
    - colour: green
    - shape: thin and tall
    - season: spring
    - objects: tall plants, tall carvings, tall lamps, images of leaves or plants

2. Fire
    - colour: red
    - shape: triangle and sharp
    - season: summer
    - objects: candles, pointed objects, red everything, actual fire, bling

3. Earth
    - colour: tan, yellow, caramel, clay, rust, brown
    - shape: squares and rectangles
    - season: late summer
    - objects: clay pots or dishes, tumbled stones, dirt or earth, granite, stones, rocks

4. Metal
    - colour: white and grey
    - shape: oval or round
    - season: autumn
    - objects: glass, mirrors, round dishes, brass pots, gold and silver jewellery, metal sculptures

5. Water
    - colour: dark blue or black
    - shape: wavy
    - season: winter
    - objects: actual water, fountains, wavy patterns in floor mats, book covers or knick-knacks

Note: Some items can represent more than one element or amplify the representation of that element. For example, a round blue vase will represent both metal and water. A red candle will represent double the fire.

THE FIVE ELEMENTS

- Wood
- Fire
- Earth
- Metal
- Water

A clay bowl with glass stones and a tea light can represent earth, metal and fire. A glass vase with water and tall flowers can represent water, metal and wood.

Reader Challenge

Pay attention to the keys areas where you spend most of your time. Each item in these areas can either support you, or not. Are the items in these prime spaces able to positively influence your mood and aid in productivity?

Combining these tools

We can now use these two tools, the bagua and the five elements, to get you started in understanding how to improve your physical workspace. The five elements are placed onto the bagua in a specific order, with each element connected with a different life area.

These elements can be used to support your goals in each life area.

The *family area* is associated with strength and support. Family dynamics are important in your corporate family as well. Honesty, trust and reliability are crucial for a family (or a corporate team) in order to leave a legacy. This area is associated with the wood element, as it is constantly growing and changing. Tall columns, trees and plants all support the wood element and growing, solid relationships. The following suggestions can help you strengthen your family area:

- Display activities or projects that support team or family spirits and encourage participation.
- Green is the colour for growth. Green in general is a soothing, supportive colour.
- Tall is the shape—use floor lamps, flagpoles, tall ferns or vertical stripes.

- Support this area with anything that is perceived as high quality, respectful of family ties, history, growth and abundance.

The **wealth and abundance area** is also associated with the wood element, tall columnar shapes, and the colours green and red. The wood element and its growth is stronger in the spring when the air is fresh and the vegetation all around you is bursting with tremendous energy. By bringing in tall items, you can reinforce the growth and abundance energy in your world. Also refer to the family area above. The following suggestions can help you strengthen your wealth and abundance area:

- This is a great area for a plant. Ideally, you want something tall and, if possible, enhanced with a flower, berry or the colour red. If you are not a plant person, consider *a representation* of plants. Silk flowers or nicely made synthetics can represent the image of plants and growth. An image of a healthy garden is also very supportive. **Please do not consider placing dried or "dead" flowers at your desk or in your home.
- Other items that represent wealth include anything of value to *you*, monetarily or sentimentally, that represents the cause. Options may include antiques, coins, pictures or carvings and artwork.
- Another option is to look ahead. Place a picture of where you want to take your next vacation or something that could motivate you to fulfill a goal, such as buying a boat, going fishing or travelling. Choose your own goal but put some sort of incentive in your corner.
- The water-element also supports growth in this area. It's okay to add a desk fountain, a seascape or blue details to foster growth.

Refer to Chapter 8 -Finding the Wealth, to expand on this area.

The ***fame and reputation area*** not only represents personal achievements; it can reflect your reputation in the world by others. Fame is associated with the fire element. You can have a strong fame area even if you feel you are very humble. The colour red is dominant in this area. The triangle shape is used here and

includes other pointed or sharp shapes. To attract attention, this is a great place to hang your sign, logo or bright lights. The following suggestions can help you strengthen your fame and reputation area:

- Use this area to display any and your most recent items of achievement. Some certificates have a red seal on them (bonus), or you may like to display them in a red frame. Display any achievements you have earned. Get them out of the drawers and into your space.
- Any items with a triangular shape or sharp dramatic lines can represent the fire element. Some clocks come in a triangle shape, candles are actual fire, plants with triangular leaves, a Kleenex box with a geometric design or a sailboat—it's all good!
- Animals are also representative of the fire element, as they are alive and have lively energy. You may use animal prints, textiles or photos in this area.

The images on the following pages show examples that can be utilized in several life areas. They could represent wealth, fame, relationships, family, wealth or health, depending on what each image means to you.

The Feng Shui Advantage

Similar pairings of ceramics and wall images can support many areas; incorporate additional enhancements from images in the picture.

Stained glass in a window can refract light and gather attention. This little red bird can enhance Wealth or Fame areas. For the Relationship area, you'll need two birds.

Ceramic fish on a wall can strengthen Wealth and Career areas.

The Feng Shui Advantage

Round things can represent Children, Creativity or Spirituality in Helpful People and Travel. Arrange similar items that have different heights for interest.

Support a closer connection using current photos reflecting happy memories in the Relationship Area.

Clay items will support the Earth element: Relationships, Health and Knowledge. Wavy lines, representing water, will support your Career. Get creative with your intentions and your enhancements!

Plants and flowers are great enhancements, either inside or out.

The Feng Shui Advantage

Choose objects and images that can strengthen your passion in life. A lovely goddess walking through a garden can be spiritual and motivating.

The **relationship area** generally refers to your personal life. At work, this area affects your close working relationships with your coworkers or partners. It is obviously important to keep this area strong. The relationship area is associated with the earth element and the key shapes are squares and rectangles. A key word here is *receptive*: Whether you are looking for a relationship or are in a relationship, you need to be able to give and receive. Display a current image of you and your spouse or partner during happy times; so you don't ever forget your commitment and dedication to another!

The following suggestions can help you strengthen your relationship area:

- This is a great area to display any earth-type objects. Things like clay pots, ceramic coffee mugs, tumbled stones or even a combination of a few things will work. Incorporate these items into holders for pens and office supplies.
- Square items are auspicious in this area, you'll need solid and grounding things such as books, folders or file boxes. Colours to use would be anything tan, caramel, rust, clay or brown. Think of autumn colours. The dark brown colour can remind us of stability, well grounded and safe.
- If you're married, it is important to have a photo of you and your partner—and *only* the two of you. This is reminder/validation that you are connected to one another and a reminder that you have support on your journey through life. Be aware that if you have a picture of only your partner, you may feel guilty seeing him or her alone at home waiting for you.
- If you are looking for a companion or more strength in an existing relationship, the key number is *two*. Try to set up items in twos: two pictures, two things in a picture, two file folders, two plants, two candles, two … you get it. This gets your brain thinking and always referring to *two* rather than just *one*.

The **children and creativity area** helps you find joy in your life. This area is intended to bring out your playful side and your imagination. It is associated with the colours white or grey, circular shapes and all types of metal. The metal element is also represented by glass, mirrors and shiny surfaces. You don't need to have children, there is still your inner child to play with. You need to have fun; find creative ways to solve daily puzzles and manoeuvre through the obstacles of life. The following suggestions can help you strengthen the children and creativity area:

- This is a great place to display artwork or other achievements by you or your child.
- The colours grey and white represent a blank canvas on which to create. Just as a chef displays culinary creations on a white plate, an artist uses a blank canvas and a doctor wears a white coat, white helps you maintain a neutral, open mind.
- Other enhancements you can use for reinforcing this area are brass pots, mirrors or circular patterns on textiles or a rug.

The ***helpful-people and travel area*** is also associated with the metal element. This is one of the most interactive areas, where you relate to the outside world, your clients and other supports. Think of a time when you were travelling and you needed help. Think of a time where you did a 'good deed for the day'. It is a great feeling. Where would we be without interaction with other humans? Remember, what goes around comes around. The following suggestions can help you strengthen your helpful-people and travel area:

- This is the place to collect items to delegate to others. Your partner or assistant, if you have one, can process the files and correspondence. These items should be placed in the near right of your doorway or entrance.
- If you have a spiritual nature, this area of your workspace is also the best place for religious books or pictures on the wall.
- Also, this is a location for your affirmations or gifts from a mentor. Photographs of meaningful places you've travelled can also be displayed in this area.
- Placing your upcoming itinerary and plane tickets here in your desk drawer can ensure you meet the right people at the right time at your destination.

Kathryn Wilking

Vacation pictures and souvenirs are fun! Display them in the Helpful People and Travel Area or any other area that makes sense to you.

The *career and life-path area* is something you need to do solo. It involves direction, fulfillment and inner exploration to find your career path. It is as individual as each day. This is associated with the water element and is intended, like deep water, to slow you down and allow you to explore the unfolding of your destiny. Courage is the key word. It takes courage to wander off the beaten track, try something new and follow the career path that calls to you.

The following suggestions can help you strengthen your career and life-path area:

- Firm grounding is important. At your desk, use a blotter. In your office, check that your chair moves easily and your feet are not blocked by stuff under your desk. At your front entrance, put down a new dark blue or black welcome mat.
- Use water related features to enhance this area. Think about stability in your choices. This is the spot for water that is contained, such as a desk fountain or aquarium. You could also choose artwork depicting healthy bodies of water: pools, lakes and ocean.
- Other items can feature a wavy pattern—on a vase, a floor mat or textiles.

> FYI: Ultimate Wealth and Prosperity is directly represented by water!

The *knowledge and self-cultivation area* transforms your knowledge and adventures into wisdom. To be wise, you need quiet time to balance your active time, to honour the full rhythm of life. This area is associated with the earth element, which encompasses grounding, logic and nurturing. It is represented by the square and rectangular shapes as well as the earth colours. The following suggestions can help you strengthen your knowledge and self-cultivation area:

- This is the best place for a library or a bookshelf. Books, CDs and resource materials that you are currently studying are all square-shaped, and they all contain knowledge. Paper items and expired resources often hang around long after they are useful. Pass them along before their condition deteriorates.
- Set up a desk or reading area in this corner of the office where you can spread out a map or make plans to engage with your hobbies or projects.
- Clay pots, tumbled stones and natural sculptures utilize the earth element and fit here nicely. Any type of earth-related gem or mineral can be displayed here.
- Display art that portrays strong mountains, quiet places and pictures of people you consider to be accomplished.

The ***health area*** is in the middle of everything. This makes logical sense, because without your health, you do not have the energy to live purposefully. Health is associated with the earth element and everything else. To strengthen this area, use colours of the earth spectrum that feel good to you. The square or rectangle shape is important to utilize, as it defines a balanced area. Earth can be represented with clay, granite, slate and tumbled stones or dirt. Wear earth colours in any spectrum of tan, caramel, rust, clay and brown. Ideally, this area should be represented by all of the five elements. The following suggestions can help you strengthen your health area:

- Yellow is a great colour for morale as it represents the sun. You can add this into your day by using yellow sticky notes (you'll never lose them), yellow notepads, yellow flowers...you get the gist.
- A greeting card with a picture of flowers or birds is another idea; anything that depicts life, vitality and good health. You can tape it down flat on your desk

in your health area or incorporate an image into your screen saver or mouse pad.
- Choose a bright, lively cushion for your chair. A favourite coffee mug can give you a supportive message.
- Place an arrangement on your desk that represents all five elements.

More enhancements about decor are in Chapter 8.

The suggestions above are easy, tangible modifications that organize and balance the chi energy in your space. It's best not to work on all nine areas of life at one time. By working on two to three related areas, you can create the momentum required to make a change. Some suggestions would be to work on the **career and wealth areas** together, or **relationships and family**. Whatever you decide to work on first is fine. This is not magic; it is positive and progressive. The energy you use to make clear intentions for change will be noticed by someone out there, and this alone will be a positive influence. The rewards will come.

The intent is to find a level of balance in your life areas. Write yourself a note to check into your life areas regularly and make any adjustments in order to meet your goals. The world is constantly moving and shifting, and you need to respond to the shifts.

The successes in your office world will be affected by the goals you have for yourself both at the office and in your personal life. When you make a decision with intention for change, you will change the energy.

Don't be surprised if some exciting changes start to happen!

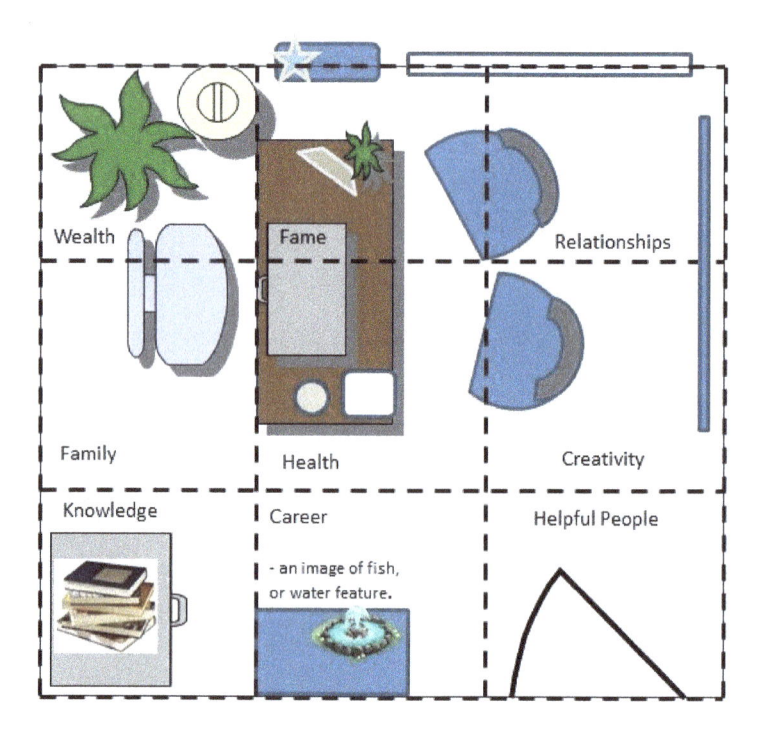

Figure 3.5 This Bagua is applied to a personal office. The person who sits here has *enhanced* her Wealth Area and Career Area to help support her goals. Many of the other areas are also reinforced.
- The Wealth Area, a *Wood element*, has a tall plant and a tall lamp.
- The Career Area, a *Water element,* has a water feature.
- The Fame Area has her achievements and awards displayed.
- The Knowledge Area is supported by shelves and square shapes.
- The artwork in Relationships/Creativity is calming and supports her personal goals.

4 The PEP Quiz: Personal Element Profile

There are lucky people who seem to have a great job and a wonderful spouse and have it all together. On the flip side, there are ones who are stressed or struggling, processing their day over-and-over and promising to do better. Yet, by simply figuring out who said what and who may be to blame, they are still not completely solving the problem.

When we are on top of the world and things are going great, we can settle in to being 'in our element'. Balancing your life starts with learning who you are and how you fit in. You need to know how to choose your position, how you fit into the team and how to choose your team or partner. Knowing your dominant element can help with this. So it is time to expand your new knowledge of the five elements with a good look at your habits and patterns.

The five elements are each assigned an auspicious number, a colour, a body part, a shape, a season, a personality and more. They have great significance in Feng Shui.

As you saw in the last chapter, the five elements relate to the basic components defined in Feng Shui: wood, fire, earth, metal and water. Their unique strengths and properties can help you manoeuvre through your day. When you have determined your **dominant element**, you can start looking at more characteristics of this element to influence and support your life. This can include selecting colours and patterns for your wardrobe, choosing a home and possessions that resonate with you or influencing team members and delegating to employees.

Kathryn Wilking

Page1 of PEP Quiz - Personal Element Profile

Do you know your **Personal Element Profile**? According to Feng Shui, your personality can be related to one of these **Five Elements**. These lists can indicate your strengths in one area or another. Check all that applies to your to find your dominant element! Can you see any friends or coworkers?

WOOD
- Flexible Schedule
- Gets things done quickly
- Loves a challenge
- Goal Oriented
- Can be Impulsive
- Enjoys a change in routine
- Confident
- Thinks BIG
- Impatient; "Get to the point!"
- Likes to wear green

FIRE
- Life of the Party
- Thinks outside the Box
- Takes control of any problem
- Animated and creative
- Relaxed approach to life
- Makes friends easily
- Wide social circle
- Passionate about life
- Drama Queen at times
- Loves to decorate for the holidays

EARTH
- Well grounded
- Reliable and trustworthy
- Happy to Compromise
- Great Nurturer
- Great Mediator
- Asks a lot of Questions
- THE contact for family and friends; the nucleus
- Compiler of people and details/bills/history/facts
- Protective of family
- Likes to wear earth tones

Page 2 of PEP Quiz - Personal Element Profile

METAL
- Precise thinker
- Sense of Justice
- Speaks UP
- Follows the Rules
- Strong Morals
- Thinks in B&W, no compromising
- Has systems in place; wills/bills/security
- All furniture/objects are squared off neatly
- Sense of humour is lacking
- Does not like to hug

WATER
- Wise, pontificating
- Excels in specialized knowledge
- Very smart and well read
- Seeks the truth, a visionary
- Reflective
- Solitary, loner
- Sly sense of humour; blunt/cruel
- Secretive, private person
- Eccentric, anti-social
- Armchair Traveller

TOTALS

WOOD _____

FIRE _____

EARTH _____

METAL _____

WATER _____

There are no right or wrong answers to this quiz.

The Element with the highest score should be your Dominant Element. Lower scores in other areas will show you have a talent to embrace a wide range of characteristics, which in turn will help make you become a well – rounded individual.

Being a unique character, you have a unique way of getting what you want in this world!

Personal Element Profile (PEP) Quiz copyright Kathryn Wilking Designs.
Evaluations using PEP are solely for the purpose of demonstrating the concepts in this book.
For comprehensive evaluations, please refer to a Certified Feng Shui consultant.
Kathryn Wilking Designs; Your Feng Shui Consultant for Safe and Happy Environments
www.kathrynwilking.com

The Personal Element Profile (PEP) Quiz in this chapter was initially designed as a game when I was asked to speak about Feng Shui to ladies' groups. It is a great icebreaker. This self-profile quiz seems to get people talking and chuckling with each other about their idiosyncrasies. It puts everyone in a good mood.

You'll need to take the PEP test to determine a starting point to find your dominant element. As there are no right or wrong answers, you may find that your dominant element will reflect your actions and position in the way you respond to others. It is very common to find that your dominant element is different in your home and working environments.

Having that awareness helps you define your friends and will give you realistic objectives to strive for in the future. You may find areas for self-improvement and become able to change your behaviour pattern with a particular person or situation.

By identifying our individualities, we could be present in our element more often. We can all learn to have good days. Could it be possible that we, on the planet Earth, could be in our element every day? Could we all learn to get along with everyone else?

Please take the time to take the PEP quiz before you read further. The PEP Quiz is on the next page and also in the back of this book –for friends and family. This is a preliminary evaluation only, and as you read more, you will fine-tune the evaluation of yourself. You will definitely use your new knowledge and use these elements to help you grow through life.

In Your Element

When you've completed the Personal Element Profile, you should have a starting point as to what your dominant element could be. If you find yourself spread across more than one element, it indicates you are flexible in different situations. For example, if you find your dominant element is metal, you can still have characteristics that show up in wood or earth elements. You may also find your dominant element at work at is very different from how you function at home.

When you find yourself confident, fulfilled, productive, energized and generally happy in a situation, take note. You're in your element, and *that* is where you need to be. We all naturally gravitate toward our comfort zone, where our natural talents lie and things are easy for us. By identifying your strengths and weaknesses in various areas, you can work toward a balance to be in your element. The results can be extremely rewarding.

> **FYI**: I flew into Calgary, Alberta where I took this deep dive to learn about the Five Elements and Personalities. It was a small group. We did our own PEP QUIZ and were encouraged to focus into behaviors from other people in our lives: bosses, coworkers, siblings and parents. I actually jumped up in the meeting with my 'AHA Moment' for this book!

This chapter is going to give you more details on the five elements so that you can identify different personality traits in your friends and coworkers. As you continue to look around and figure out what makes you tick, you can see why your relationships with some people are very different from others.

A Solopreneur or an Entrepreneur wears many hats in a day and will require skills in many elements to function, as they need to be well-rounded. Hire or delegate tasks to those who have skills in your weaker areas.

By taking the time to identify the elements of the people around you, you will be able to connect patterns in your behaviour with certain element types. Just as we need to function 'wearing many hats', learning how to get along with everyone is an acquired skill. Once you attain it, you can manoeuvre through the workplace harmoniously with your coworkers.

Wood People

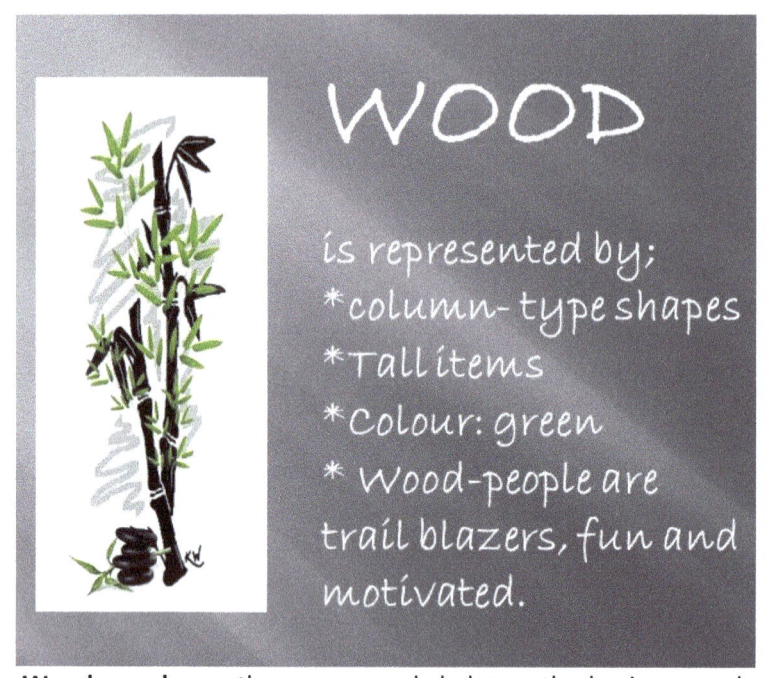

WOOD

is represented by:
* column-type shapes
* Tall items
* Colour: green
* Wood-people are trail blazers, fun and motivated.

Wood people are the movers and shakers—the busiest people around! They have great ideas, they have energy, and they have the means to make it happen! Yes! Yes! And, yes, they *do* like to use *lots* of exclamation marks!

If you want the job done, give the task to the busiest person—a person whose dominant element is wood.

The wood element is represented by the season of springtime—a time of growth, high energy and the colour green. There is fresh abundance in the air and new birth of the deciduous trees, flowers, birds and insects. It'll feel like a newfound energy in the universe. Wood people will find their task lists growing and their days filled with great ideas and good causes to support.

Wood people tend to be well-balanced, likeable individuals. They are fast learners and have a strong foundation on which to stand in order to succeed. They like to dive in and get things done quickly. They tend to be confident, result-oriented, competitive risk-takers. They love to see a project through to the end, and many become very powerful in their profession.

Common professions for wood people include:

- sales, any and all sectors
- customer service
- real estate
- wedding planner
- entrepreneur
- small business owner
- travel services
- set designer
- advertising/marketing

If you are a wood person, you enjoy lots of energy, unlimited growth and great rewards working with other wood people. Being an extrovert, you have the ability to easily connect with people, gather them together and work towards a cause.

Many wood people are so good at organizing and delegating, they may even forget to finish the job—because they are already on to the next one. Other behaviours common to wood people:

- Their desk and office could appear to be out of control. They like to see everything, and they like to know where everything is. They prefer to keep things within reach.

- They have a lot of projects on the go. They tend to change the subject quickly and then come back with questions when processing information.

- They often interrupt and like to keep the conversation moving: "Get to the point!"

- Their resting area (personal space) tends to have a plethora of hobbies, books and "things to do" to keep busy.
- Some tend to clean up and get rid of things too quickly. An item needs to have a purpose or it gets moved to the trash. Their motto: "Outta-sight, outta-mind."

Wood children are often rewarded for being self-starters or natural leaders. While rising to the top of their class, they are often misunderstood by their young friends. Their vocabulary and problem-solving skills can be mature for their age.

As a young child, wood people were probably disciplined for speaking out and standing up for themselves. In fact, they were probably disciplined for being too much of everything—too demanding, too loud, too reckless and too competitive. The irony is that many of these qualities are survival skills they require as adults.

Real Snapshots

The real snapshots following this and subsequent element descriptions are taken from real life. Although the examples are not solely from the workplace, the characteristic behaviours can help you identify these elements, sometimes in their extreme form. The names and some of the professions have been altered to protect each person's identity.

Meg, a wood child full of energy, wanted to experience life to the fullest. She was constantly put down for being too loud and too reckless. She was always the one taken in for stitches as a result of taking risks on the playground. Sifting through her life lessons, she remembers being told to sit down and shut up. She felt her childhood was very stifling.

A busy, fun-loving gal, she had no problem finding work or attracting friends and boyfriends. It is odd that with all these people and acquaintances, she still wasn't fulfilled in life. Meg was always three steps ahead of everybody. Two marriages later, she finally met a guy who can keep up with her, and with this security, she has been able to settle into her career. Meg is still a busy, wood person who has projects on the go constantly.

Donna, a retail salesperson for office services, started out as a part-time employee. She was focused on getting ahead and moved quickly into a supervisor position and then became a regional manager. Never taking the time for a personal life, she excelled in her job performance and received many achievement awards for her successes. Nearing retirement, she was apprehensive about what to do when the time came to slow down. Always ahead of her time, Donna launched a brand-new consulting business on the eve of retirement, wrote a book and is now running training seminars throughout the year—an energetic achievement for anyone and impressive for a lady in her sixties! It is tough to tell a wood person when it is time to stop or slow down.

Joe grew up with a lot of ideas and a lot of energy. I recall Joe as a youngster; he wanted to get out there and travel the world. Too busy to sit still and attend college or university, he jumped from job to job trying to find himself.

When following up with one of Joe's family at an event, I learned he'd been overseas for a few years. When he first left North America, he drove a huge harvester combine in Australia for one of the farms and then moved on to Southeast Asia to teach English as a Second Language. He is now running his own tour company out of East Asia; validating wood energy—the movers and shakers.

Fire People

FIRE is represented by:
* triangular shapes
* sharp or bright objects
* Colour: Red
* Fire-people are lively, passionate and energized

Fire people are not only on fire; they love the fame that goes with the territory. They crave recognition for being the hero, the one with the great ideas or the one who remembered the chocolate cake for the office birthday. They are insightful, full of problem-solving skills and passionate about life.

Fire people like to think outside the box. They like to have fun and have a wide social circle on which to bounce off their ideas. They are understanding, courteous and generally do not hold a grudge.

Fire people may also have a reputation for being dramatic and can overreact in any situation at hand. In some cases, they can be rather high-maintenance, consuming other people's time and energy. Fire people are *out there*. While you may only think of celebrities as examples of fire people, there are many right in your own neighbourhood.

Many of us are looking for recognition or fame on a project and don't necessarily need to be the star of the show. If someone asks a question or stand up for a cause, I call this a 'fire moment'. Don't play shy. We ALL need to voice an opinion and be noticed!

Some likely occupations for true fire people:

- actor/actress
- lecturer
- musician
- politician
- preacher
- stand-up comic
- newscaster
- entrepreneur
- podcaster
- webinar host

If you are a fire person, you have energy and passion. You are the one with the social life, lots of followers and seem to have a lot of fun in your life—the more bling, the better. You tend to wear bright colours and are relatively open-minded, with good problem-solving skills.

This fire individual might like to arrive late (on purpose), make an entrance and get attention by interrupting the scene. In other cases, the fire element shows up in the form of anger. The person who has a bad temper or loud behaviour can be extremely disruptive.

Here are other behaviours common to fire people:

- They like to entertain and love the energy that guests bring. They like dramatic, bold colour schemes.

- Often shopaholics, they like new clothes and shoes. They will dress with the mood of the day and require praise and reinforcement for their choices.

- They will keep their favourite things in sight and show them off: "This is my …" and "This is what we picked up in …."

- They can be messy and disorganized, with many unfinished projects on the go.

- They seem to be either inspired and passionate or burned out. They may have no way to balance emotions.

- They will display their awards, acknowledgments and pictures with famous people in prominent places, justifying their presence.

- They will always have a wild story to tell about their experiences with the dry-cleaner, a hotel, fitness club, etc. They enjoy playing the victim in these situations.

- Many true fire people do not appear to have an off switch, as they give 110 percent daily to the task at hand.

Fire children are often rewarded for making friends easily and brightening people's day with their joyful exuberance. They are happy to be around other people and crave attention for doing well in performing arts—school plays, gymnastics, dancing or singing.

As a young child, fire people were probably disciplined for talking too fast. They are busy people, grabbing the attention from all the other kids. Appearing to be a bit scatterbrained, they can bounce between making light of some situations and providing a dramatic performance in others. Inconsistency with friendships could lead to isolation and disappointment, which could in turn lead to another dramatic performance.

Wood people and fire people are both outgoing. Although they get along, they often seek quieter individuals for a long-term partnership.

Real Snapshots

Henry, a corporate executive for a large global company, was in fire mode all the time. He was a polished individual, loved by his family, and he would do just about anything for his four kids. He loved to talk and entertain.

Henry would start by asking about your latest vacation and then proceed to tell you all about *his* vacation. He would try to corner you into a political discussion, and when you decided not to talk politics, he'd tell you about his opinion anyway and how he could solve the worlds' problems.

Don, reassigned from his high-profile (fire person) position in politics, was adjusting to the new environment of having a lesser position. He would wander over to other people's workstations just to chat and offer unsolicited advice. His favourite 'catch' was to say something like, "Well, I'm glad *that* is finished!" This would invite someone to inquire "What's finished?" Another favourite of his was, "Have you seen Joe lately? Do you want to know what he's been doing on the 14th floor?" Don, always a nice guy, would be happy to share his knowledge with you about what was going on. After a while, people began to distrust him—too much gossip and drama about other people.

Patrick, a tradesperson in his fifties, decided this was the year to renovate his own home. A perfectionist in his trade, he made sure this house would have the best materials. He forged ahead assembling the best team, purchasing the best copper piping, the best hardwood flooring, the best windows. And yet, there were some issues with his obsession to build the best house that he failed to foresee. It was his wife who went to the bank to finance the renovation. In fact, she had to refinance three times over the next two years in order to continue the process, as Patrick ripped out every wall and stairwell in his master plan to 'make it the best.' His income suffered as he took more time to work on the house. The wife's income was stable, but they were maxed out on their loan payments and credit cards. They were living with their two kids in a house under construction for years. No one was happy. Fire people can be driven and consumed in their tasks, so much that they can destroy what they have built.

Mary, a young 50-ish Entrepreneur logged into Virtual Marketing Groups with obsession over the internet, chatting people up and making new contacts. Although the idea is to promote your business and (hopefully) help support other businesses, Mary was quite one-sided. People soon got tired of motivating texts sent after hours and posting images of her working out at the gym. ("See how amazing I look today.") Fire people can be fun and amazing, and yet, if your audience or clients are not on board, these efforts and 'support' can be misrepresented.

> On one side of the cycle we have the extroverts: wood people and fire people. They are both social beings and enjoy the excitement in the world.
>
> Metal people and water people are introverts. They are the ones who follow the rules and hold up moral values in society.
>
> And then, we have earth people who are in the middle and they like it that way! The earth people are the best arbitrators; a neutral force insisting that everyone get along.

Earth People

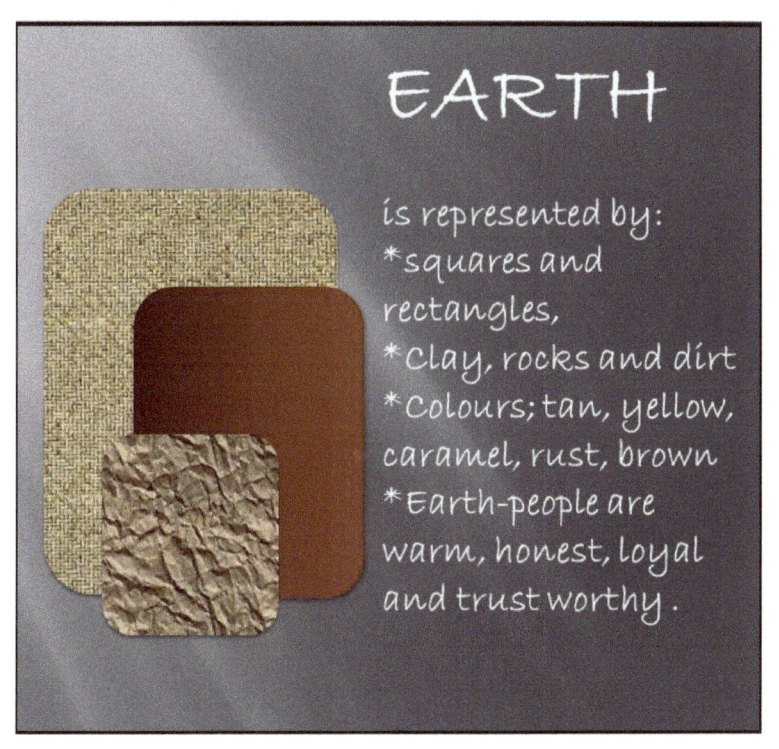

> # EARTH
>
> is represented by:
> *squares and rectangles,
> *Clay, rocks and dirt
> *Colours; tan, yellow, caramel, rust, brown
> *Earth-people are warm, honest, loyal and trustworthy.

Earth people are down to earth, trustworthy and sincere. They would give you the shirt off their back if they could, and they are loyal to a fault at times. Earth people are the mediators, the arbitrators and the coordinators of the family and workplace. They are detail-oriented, diplomatic, kind and nurturing. They are the type of employee who likes to please others. They often morph into the role of a trainer for new hires or the go-to for anything in the company. As the nucleus of the family, they are the curators of the information they've collected in order to stay in touch with family, ancestors and high-school chums. Every association and family needs an earth person.

Some likely professions for earth people include:

- nurse
- secretary
- administrative assistant AA
- virtual assistant VA
- customer service
- school teacher
- childcare worker
- chef – food industry
- pharmacist
- pet-care worker

If you are an earth person, you are seen as a quiet, humble person wearing casual, comfortable clothes. You are reliable, detail-oriented and a great moderator for harmony. You are the one juggling the committee meetings, carpools and PTA meetings. Some earth people burn out because they cannot say no to any and all demands placed on them. Other behaviours common to earth people:

- They like to collect things. Their environment is often cluttered with papers, recipes, books, journals and magazines.

- They always have a full pantry for entertaining anyone who walks in the door. They best connect with and nurture others while in the kitchen.

- As collectors of antiques and nostalgia, they love to read memoirs and experience history.

- They like textiles, such as blankets, pillows, tablecloths and draperies. They tend to decorate with small muted patterns and soft colours.

- They have an easygoing personality and cannot say no to those they feel loyal to.

- In extreme cases, they can become meddlesome or manipulative, as they need to be needed. The empty-nest syndrome can be very difficult for these people.

- They can be easily diverted and love to go where a need is perceived.

- True peacemakers, they always get into the middle of a confrontation—first to understand the problem and then to keep the peace.

- Comfort is the number-one priority—comfort foods, comfortable beds, comfortable temperatures.

Earth children are often rewarded for being practical when dealing with money and thinking ahead. Their kind and easygoing nature comes with a barrage of questions, trying to understand how the world works. They are mature for their age and make great mom-helpers, helping with younger siblings.

As young children, earth people were probably disciplined for sticking their nose in where it didn't belong. They can become shy or sensitive toward the activities they don't understand. Some earth children become quite bossy trying to maintain order on the playground when the group doesn't want to follow the rules of the game.

Real Snapshots

Ellen, a lovely gal in western Canada, is a seamless blend of earth and metal elements. Marrying later in life and having no children of her own, Ellen carved a name out for herself as a teacher of Home Economics. She was precise, inquisitive and a perfectionist, whether baking in the kitchen, sewing or knitting, or painting designs on garden furniture. When she married Ryan, he came with a grown daughter and two grandchildren. Not only did she have the earth-mama role down to a science, but later, she ended up fascinated by genealogy on both sides of the family. Her retirement years are spent head down in papers, writing to extended family members, compiling memory books and scanning the documents and photos to leave to the next generation. She is so busy and so happy to have this project to do! To see her workspace, you'd think she was running the country. Every pile has a purpose, and she knows *exactly* where everything is. (Typical earth person.)

Ekaterina, a middle-aged Polish lady I met years ago, was a typical stereotype of a Polish 'earth mama'. Although she was a scientist at a research facility, she would always rush home to cook lunch for her grown boys. I asked her, "Ekaterina, your boys are in their twenties. Why do you feel compelled to rush home to cook lunch for them?" And dinner? And more? There was no discussion. If she fed her boys well, they could concentrate on their studies. That was what she wanted to do and what she needed to do.

James is also an 'earth mama'. While this roll is expected in females, many accomplished men also have this as a dominant element. James learned to bake while working at a bakery during his university years. Learning to make pies, buns and bread in the wee hours of the morning was a great job for a student. Now older, James still enjoys cooking and baking as a balance from the tasks of his business. He is quite relaxed making multiple pies for a group of friends.

> People with earth qualities don't need to be parents.
>
> There are many hobbies and professions that can cultivate compassion, kindness and joy in other ways.
>
> You'll find these wonderful people working with food, plants, animals, gardening, the environment, as well as children; giving their time and energy freely.

Metal People

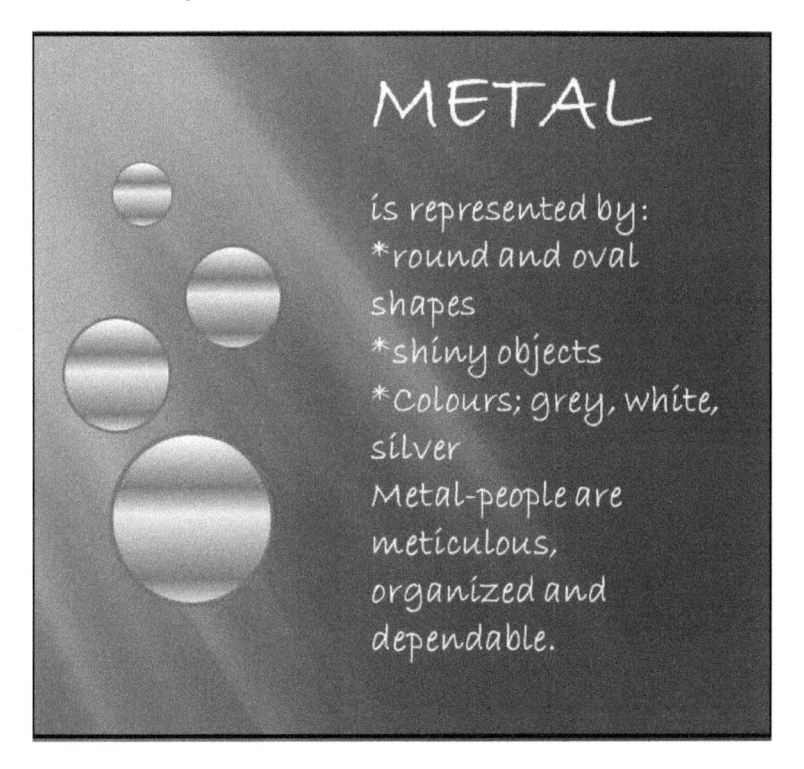

> **METAL**
>
> is represented by:
> *round and oval shapes
> *shiny objects
> *Colours; grey, white, silver
>
> Metal-people are meticulous, organized and dependable.

Metal people tend to be a little more introverted than their coworkers. They think in black and white, follow the rules and have an extreme sense of justice. They exhibit precise thinking and are not easily distracted once they get started on a project. They are strong to speak up when someone is bending the rules or trying to instigate a shortcut. They do not fare well with change. They like order, rules and numbers because these are finite and easy to understand. Metal people can be overly analytical and stubborn in situations where they have chosen to stand their ground.

Anywhere that rules, policy or procedures are involved, you'll find a metal person. In work mode, these individuals have a limited sense of humour; they are all business.

Some likely professions for metal people:

- doctor
- lawyer
- computer geek/analyst
- bookkeeper
- accountant
- bank teller
- draftsperson
- medical illustrator
- law enforcement
- electrician
- plumber
- engineer
- biologist

If you are a metal person, your shirt will likely be tucked in neatly and the buttons done right up close to the neck. You will always present yourself as very organized, composed and professional. A perfectionist with numbers and technology, you will always have the answers.

Another interesting characteristic of metal people is their creative edge. Some develop their skills as fine artists, tradespeople and other jobs that require commitment, accuracy and exactness. Their problem-solving skills show up here with obsessive precision.

Other behaviours common to metal people:

- They can be overly cautious and analytical, as they have trust issues with new concepts and new people.

- They tend to think only with right or wrong answers, which makes them hard to deal with in negotiations.

- Introverted and self-sufficient, they work best on projects by themselves.

- They are perfectionists who require a plan that is detail-oriented, organized and feasible.
- Having strong morals and integrity, they will speak up when injustice is suspected.
- They live by the rules and the policy and procedures of the company.
- Their furniture and possessions will be lined up and squared off into neat spaces.
- They will probably not display private-life pictures or knick-knacks at their desk. Their workspace will always be tidy and clean.

Metal children are often rewarded for acting mature and grown-up. They play independently and keep their bedrooms neat and orderly. These kids are trustworthy and will follow the rules set out for them.

As young children, metal people were probably thought of as being too serious. They didn't have a lot of friends so were often left in their own world with their own odd games and explorations. They could be difficult when adapting to any change in routine or change in the seasons. Metal kids can be picky eaters and most refuse to try something new.

Real Snapshots

Rick, a lawyer, is a typical metal person. He is sceptical and analytical about everything and is indifferent to casual talk. With no need for small talk, he lives with and reacts to whatever he is focusing on that day. Rick is engrossed with his clients, fully dedicated and caring about the impact of the results of their cases. He is focused.

Lily had all the cards lined up for success. She was identified as gifted as a child and therefore encouraged and praised throughout her elementary and high-school years. She went to the local university to study accounting and emerged at the top of her class. This is a good career choice for a metal person.

As time went on, Lily found it more and more difficult to get along with her coworkers. She eventually got fired. She took the company to court for wrongful dismissal and won. This sequence repeated itself several times over the next few years, with Lily always playing the victim and then suing her employer. She was unable to listen to another point of view, and vocalized that she was always right. (This example is recognized as metal with fire-element moments.)

Caroline was a veteran in her industry, and all its products and procedures were second nature to her. The office manager would send new hires to her for instructions. Caroline's lack of patience for the newbies was apparent by the brash way she spoke to them all. She fumed each day with a lack of respect; "I'll do it for you" or "I'm checking to see if you are doing it right."

Caroline's department had a high turnover of employees, as the new hires requested transfers. Caroline was frustrated and finally told Human Resources that whenever she came in to work she felt like she was preparing for a fight.

A metal person is not the one to nurture and support new staff members, no matter how much experience he or she may have. Caroline was eventually fired. Both Caroline and HR should have addressed these issues years earlier.

Water People

> **WATER**
>
> is represented by:
> *wavy shapes
> *water or water-type features
> *Colours; dark blue or black
> Water-people are calm, sedentary introverts.

It is common for senior citizens to shift from a dominant element in their prime to the **water element** later in life. They have lived their lives and are quieting down, reflecting on the past. Water people have very limited social lives by choice, preferring to experience life through books and documentaries. They are very happy in their position as armchair travellers. If you compare this to swimming in deep water, true water people can actually become stuck in their lives and even be depressed. They need to think and plan out everything in advance: where to go, where to park and who is going to be there. It takes a lot of effort to change the mind of 'deep water' people, let alone get them moving.

Water people are very well read and generally succeed in a profession that deals with specific precision, similar to metal people. Their sense of humour can be somewhat distorted, dry and insulting. They are hoping to impress you with their wit and know-how, wanting to offer advice; sometimes doing a lot more harm than good. It is common for people to grow into this element as their career matures and they are able to provide calm, wise counsel or service in their chosen profession.

Common professions for water people include:

- judge
- surgeon
- banker/lender
- philosopher
- author
- physicist
- CEO- Chief Executive Officer
- Advisory Board Member

If you are a 'deep water' person, you can be identified by some of the phrases you use every day: "I can't do that" or even "You can't do that!" You take pride in thinking things through, but, have different ideas about risk and safety issues. This likely means you need to take time to think through that (inconceivable) idea. Prematurely, you often challenge simple ideas, treating them like something barbaric or catastrophic.

Water people may not commit to a faith. As deep thinkers and very private individuals, they have already figured out where they stand in the universe. Their expert knowledge will support this view.

Other behaviours common to water people:

- They can be introverted. They prefer that other people put out the effort to communicate or bring them information.
- They claim they are busy all the time, when actually they have a set routine and are not willing to alter it to accommodate others.

- They can be stingy and critical of others' spending, morals and choices.

- They will have original, imaginative ideas and then lean on others to execute them.

- They are very observant and well-read— seekers of the truth.

- They contemplate their place in the big picture of life.

- They can have difficulty with conformity, changing routine, moving offices or reshuffling the team. They could be stubborn and then retreat (not happily) when pushed into certain situations.

- They like their creature comforts: a high-end mattress, a big TV, a nice easy chair.

Water children are often rewarded for being observant and able to think through problems for themselves. Their imagination and creativity show up through their writing and projects at school, confirming that they are very smart kids.

As a young child, water people were probably disciplined for being blunt and tactless—putting others down with insults. They can be very sceptical of new surroundings, and they trust no one to enter their secretive world. This leads to suspicion and a nonconformist attitude toward the games the other children play.

I have met only a few water children. These kids, with their sober moods appear to be little adults rather than children. They may have experienced loss at a very, early age. Survival for water people in childhood often means imaginary friends and living the life of a loner.

Kathryn Wilking

Real Snapshots

Rob, a 'deep water' person, was an English gentleman. His wife died a few years before I met him and his adult children were all off leading their own lives. Long retired, he had only himself to look after.

For his 79th birthday, he bought himself a huge 48-inch flat-screen TV and a new La-Z Boy chair. Later, he added on to his cable bundle in order to watch the 'scream channel'. Why the 'scream channel'? Because he thought it was funny! Rob had all he needed in his life. He wasn't going anywhere, and no one could convince him otherwise. He was happy to be an armchair traveller and experience adventures without leaving his house.

Sue is a lady in her mid-fifties. Her frustrated relationship with her mom, a lawyer, had consumed her entire adult life. According to Sue, her mother was unappreciative of Sue's accomplishments and was generally focused on her work. Sue previously worked as a secretary for many years and catered to other people's needs (An earth person asking to be appreciated by a metal person.) She married a fellow more than 10 years older than herself. They did not have any children. Sue has been more contemplative with her life as she approaches 60 years old. Lately, she has turned into a deep water person. She cries a lot, is depressed most days and drinks a bit too much every day to cope. She seems to be stuck lingering in the past rather than seeing the great life she has now or could have in the future. Sue doesn't have the motivation to put a lot back into her work. She'll likely need counselling or therapy if she can't shake this herself. As stated earlier, it is really tough to move water people when they are stuck.

Ray was the youngest of seven children. His mom worked outside the home and his dad was a hardworking labourer. Ray was basically raised by his siblings—three older brothers and three older sisters. Without a lot of supervision in the house, Ray witnessed amazing screaming fights between his sisters and fistfights between his brothers. He confided that he often felt he was sitting on the windowsill looking in at a movie. Always the observer, he never learned to trust anyone completely.

Ray morphed into being a water person purely as a tactic for his own survival. An accomplished electrician by day and a musician at night, Ray wrapped himself up with rules and societal norms to fit in. Definitely a loner, he resisted growth and development in himself. Ray develops anxiety issues with any change in work schedules, technology or routine.

> **FYI:** Primary or dominant elements can shift as we grow.

Larry has moved through most of the five-elements in his life. He spent his early years moving from country to country with his family in an executive lifestyle. He was well-read, came from a supportive loving family and had grand ideas for forging ahead in his life. Larry was convinced he could get rich on his own life experiences and didn't need formal education (wood).

He spent the early years overriding people's opinions and authority (fire) and stepping on a few of toes along the way. He 'married the girl', had 'the kid', bought 'the house' and did everything that society told him he should. Yet, Larry never really figured out how to fit into society (metal).

After a few decades, he ended up on the beach selling ice cream, convinced that he had beat the system. He could collect a welfare check and still get paid to sell ice cream on the beach (wood, again). Larry finally gave up, hit rock bottom and received psychiatric help. He now spends his time trying to solve the world's problems from his little apartment - cynical and resentful for his lack of success (deep water).

Me: In My Element

I'd like for people to think I'm a well-rounded-element person. The truth is that I am a dominant wood person. I was trying to refrain from being labelled, but it is really tough to hide a wood personality. I naturally venture into the fire-element zone, and I do retreat into the cool water element when needed. As mentioned, well-rounded people can fit into many areas.

> **FYI**: More than 25 years ago, I married an earth-person. One of the many things we like to do together is go sailing. For me, the calmness of the water is relaxing. For Stephen, when he goes into racing mode, he morphs into a metal person. He loves to fuss on his boat: all the details, the trimmings, the technical data he uses to go faster, be better and go farther. A good finish in a race is his triumph for the day. We work well together; same sport, different agenda.

In the next chapters, I'll show how the elements are arranged in cycles and how you can use these to find support in the other elements—very practical when choosing a partner for life or for working relationships.

5   Clues to Understand People

Now that you know your element and can recognize some of the people around you, we can begin to explore how to use this knowledge. In any business or personal relationship, once you have figured out how to find clues about different, life is so much better. Let's look at what it may mean in terms of clutter-busting and productivity.

Be a Detective: learn how clutter habits can reveal the real YOU, and your spouse, kids, coworkers and more. So much FUN!

One way I figure out people's element as a starting point is to have a look at the way they file or organize their stuff: home, desk, car, etc. What do you think I'm looking for?

If I see shoes all lined up at the door, coats hung up and counters clean, I'll suspect the person-in-charge has strong, metal element traits. Metal people can be huge neat-freaks.

If I can barely open the door as there are shoes all over the place, I'll suspect this is a busy family with a lot of wood-energy. Wood people are about doing things rather than tidying.

Use the same observations for your family, coworkers and neighbours. No judgment here, just the facts. While identifying a few traits about the people closest to you, you'll better understand that person and less likely to criticize.

Learning these clues about clutter habits can also show you how to maintain the clutter in your life. The following are descriptions related to clutter and the personal element characteristics: Wood, Fire, Earth, Metal and Water.

Ever wondered why some people can thrive in a messy world, and others need a system? Read further.

Clutter Habit Clues

If you relate to the descriptions below **in only one element**, chances are this is your dominant personal element. You'll need to learn how to get along with others and their element, which will help to give you better perspective in life and the workforce.

If you relate to a few descriptions **in many elements**, you have flexibility. As well, you may be more well-rounded than others. Your strengths can be found in understanding opposites regarding relationships and cooperation.

WOOD - Wood-people are extraverts with the ability to attract many people to help with their ideas and projects. An adventurous person, you thrive on expanding ideas and new projects. You rarely say 'no' to a challenge!

Thus, your desk is usually a mess. You have high hopes; too many projects, things to read, and not enough planning time. It is time you discipline yourself to 'say no', and delegate some of the projects. Set aside a few hours in your non-scheduled day ...just to catch up, and deal with the mountain of paperwork, in-boxes, and desk-drawers. Then *purge and recycle*!

Spread everything out on the floor to see the magnitude of your problem. Sort out the projects into coloured folders (you love colours) and prioritize the ones that need attention daily, monthly, annually and the special project files.

One of the downfalls of being a wood-person is that you can burn out easily- literally! Wood-people can be impatient and 'feed fuel to the fire' working with drama-prone individuals. By cutting down on this action, and projects related with fire-people, you'll take one step towards looking after your health, and two steps towards containing the chaos on your desk.

FIRE- Fire-people are consumers…literally! You like to shop and collect dramatic things, getting attention along the way. Much of your clutter is related not just for work, but unpacked items, things that don't have a place or things you need to return.

Your motivation is to stay on top of your game, and yet, you somehow expect people to pick up after you. It will be tough for you to muster the discipline to clean up your work area. As an extravert, you are passionate about life; you'd be missing all the fun if you stay inside to do this by yourself!

The clutter on your desk is related to clutter in the closet, drawers and under the bed. Fire-people are consumers who not only consume material items, but also the energy of others around them. Take the time to look at your entire house: clean, then *purge and recycle!*

Your attention span can be short. Paying for help is suggested. If you ever burn out, which you will, you want to have a few friends left for you to hang out with, before the next fire (opportunity) comes along. You'll feel better with a clean slate, so try to imprint an image in your head of 'tidiness', so you'll be motivated to keep it that way.

EARTH - Earth-people are well grounded and well-liked for their arbitration skills. You like to collect things and 'nest' for future needs. You are a reliable source for any and all miscellaneous stuff. With all these organization skills and knowledge, you may be overwhelmed hanging onto other people's projects, files and baggage.

While protective of these items, only you know the filing system or whereabouts of all these nests. Therefore, your clutter is defining your self worth.

Earth-people tend to have hoarding qualities; not something you'd expect from a successful individual. Piles and piles of stuff tend to become stale and stagnant - resulting in a musty, dead space.

Take the initiate to *purge the piles*. Make time to re-file necessary items in a logical spot for others to fend for themselves. Remove everything that does not support you and only surround yourself with things you love.

You'll still have clutter issues, as you love to collect things, and you are very sentimental. But, try not to take over other people's space; the clutter is yours and yours alone.

METAL - Metal-people tend to be well organized and meticulous about details. You file most of your thoughts in black-or-white, resisting the pull to be flexible. Regarding clutter, you have that taken care of too: paid, filed, out-of-sight. As the back bone of a corporation, you generally will not have clutter issues, but you do need to share information with others.

The introvert in you helps to keep things organized. You have personal papers in order, licenses up to date, safety issues looked after; as well as, live by policy, rules and procedures. You are very organized, with everything in its place.

Your weakness can be social. Your pride is sustained by assurance that you know more than others.

You don't have a clutter problem, but, others do! Very frustrating! You may have to be patient and flexible trying to extract documents or information from others; it's all about cooperation and working towards the same objective.

WATER - Water-people are pontifical and like to sit back and watch things happening around them. Brilliant, and meticulous, they can be very critical towards others. Oddly combined with a cynical sense of humour, water-people are rarely social.

You tend to delegate tasks to others rather than put out an effort yourself. You resist self promotion, and harbour your successes in storage; never to be looked at and never to be disposed of...sort of locked in time. You may have collected memories, documents and files from a lifetime of exciting casework, therefore, you may not have a messy clutter-type problem, but more of a storage problem.

Your priorities are not as simple as cleaning up the desk; as reading, or gathering information gives you your edge. You relish the fact that you have the key answers –and others don't.

To keep all your clutter and storage issues under control, you may need to invest in reliable help; someone who can understand your brilliance and anti-social behavior.

Clutter Games

One of the theories of Feng Shui is that we need to 'create space' to receive more! We humans tend to hang onto things from the past or hang onto things that we 'may' be able to use in the future. Either way, our homes are stuffed with all kinds of stuff! Lifting the stuck-ness/stuffiness/bulk in our lives will certainly open up opportunities and space to receive more. Set your mind for the future to be better and more prosperous.

Think about this: Self motivation is the most powerful! Set your mind in motion! Here are a few ways to play while pairing down a few things, or tackling a HUGE purge:

1. **Lost and Found**: Each day or each week depending on the necessity:
   - Take an empty laundry basket and walk through the house picking up anything and everything that doesn't belong in each area. When you're done, this is the game: Where does everything belong?
   While taking a second walk around the house, place the 'lost items' back in their designated space.

2. **Deep Dive:** for 3 days, best for weekends:
   - The goal is to toss/remove/donate/gift/repurpose items OUT of your home. Remove 27 items from your home for 3 days. Therefore 81 items will be designate to leave! Make sure these items actually **leave** the premises.
   Tip: A box of shoes counts as ONE item.

3. **Slow Start:** a gradual purge over a month. Best to begin on the 1st of the month for easy tracking:
   - On the 1st of the month, remove one item from the home. On the second, remove two items. On the third, three items, and so on. By the 30th of the month you'll have removed 165 items! Please think this challenge through: It is not practical to drive to the Good Will Depot everyday: have a box in the garage, the trunk of your car or the porch. Your items should be half-way OUT to the curb and beyond. Plan a drop-off date.

4. **Make The Shift: a** 27 day program:
   - An interactive concept with short 5min videos is sent straight to your email each day - prompting YOU to take charge and shift the energy in 27 areas of your home. This includes your underwear drawer, refrigerator, car, bathrooms and so much more! Guaranteed to make you laugh, take action and view your space in a new light.

   More information on You Tube and the website:
   https://kathrynwilking.com/make-the-shift

Be sure to place some whimsy into your makeover!

Communications for Solving Problems

For successful communications with **wood people**:

- Firmly establish your credibility. Focus on results and get right down to business.
- Make eye contact. Wood people are a loyal, sincere group and don't have time to deal with someone they are trying to figure out.
- Keep the pace moving when presenting options and new ideas, as wood people are fast thinkers and can be way ahead of you.
- Watch for frustration; either your facts are not lined up or you are glossing over something obvious.
- They will not support you if your credibility is compromised.
- Wood people like options. When making collective decisions, give them an either-or choice so they still feel they are in control.

For successful communications with ***fire people***:

- Keep things light and fun to get their attention. They like to talk about themselves.
- Praise them and thank them for their ideas and input.

- They'll lose attention quickly if you ask too much from them in an area in which they cannot excel. And yet, they may come up with great ideas. Listen carefully.
- Proposals and solutions should be exciting and dramatic. Use colour!
- If they are getting off the topic, give them a few minutes to talk it out before bringing the conversation back to the issue at hand.
- Always follow up. They like to know that you are behind them. Be a fan!
- They can have loose loyalties and will move along.
- Hugs are okay—when initiated by them.

For successful communications with *earth people*:

- They like to feel comfortable. Offer tea, coffee or water and sit down together to make a connection; maintain full attention.
- Set the tone; small talk is a good start. Ask earth people about their family and what types of things they like to do.
- Don't rush an earth person. Leave time to process and ask more questions.
- Listen carefully. An earth person will tell you exactly what he or she wants to hear.
- Offer simple solutions to solve problems. Use good buzzwords: p*ractical, down-to-earth, recyclable, eco-friendly* and *natural*. Earth people like to think they are doing a good deed with their choices.
- Before making a decision, they want to know how everyone else could will be affected.
- Hugs are okay after you've developed a firm and mutual connection.

For successful communications with *metal people*:

- Respect the boundaries they have set. Sit where they want you to sit and leave when they want you to leave.

- Be professional and do not interrupt a metal person.
- Metal people need you to notice the detail they have put into the project and the time that went into the presentation. Just notice; do not be excessive in your praise.
- Follow the rules whether for games, chores, tasks or projects. Most guidelines have been well thought out and provide structure, so give them a try.
- Make a checklist and duplicate it so that everyone knows what each person is doing. For the metal person, this is a form of rules and provides needed guidelines.
- When dividing tasks, find an extrovert (wood or fire person) to do the public and social tasks, leaving the metal person to do the quieter ones. Everyone will be a winner.
- Do not try to hug a metal person without permission.

For successful communications with **water people**:

- Develop a rapport and trust over time.
- Give them time to think, process and digest the information before asking for an endorsement. Water people analyse things in a deep way.
- Slow down your speech when presenting new ideas. Breathe. Make sure each point gets enough consideration. Be creative and original.
- Water people like to know the big picture. Be a visionary when trying to make a point. Watch for cynical barbs and criticism; they are really asking questions.
- Develop a support network. Water people need help from others to make their dreams a reality.
- Listen for the use of a cynical tone, such as "What would you want to do *that* for?" This tone makes any discussion fall flat. The tone could actually mean, "I'm not interested" or "Don't try to convince me."

- Do not even *try* to encourage a water person to stand in the limelight. They prefer to support the cause in their own way.

Where to Tread Lightly

Wood People

In most cases, wood people pull up their socks and bounce back from adversity. They are survivors, and they have ideas and the energy to carry on. But as with all the elements, there are some things to watch out for.

A wood person's worst fear can be summed up as loss of power. As survivors, their whole mindset is leadership, to be in control. Any circumstance that involves powerlessness, helplessness or being stifled in any way is stressful. They need space in order to gather ideas and keep the momentum going. They are the first to grab the ball or a new idea and run with it. When the road is blocked or they are confused and beaten down, they don't have anywhere to grow. With loss of power and no vision, they will move on — "I'm outta here!"

Fire People

A fire person's worst fear is being cut off from an audience. A timeout, a pink slip or a layoff can lead to disaster. This derailment in a fire person's world will lead to inactivity, separation, confusion and isolation. If you intentionally upset their world, fire people will seek retaliation. They need people and will seek out approval from another source if they don't get it in their present situation.

Fire people need to learn how to control their spontaneous energy, as their antics can be very distracting to coworkers. Finding an after-hours outlet for free expression could be helpful to balance their energy in the workplace. Fire people need to recognize that most individuals they deal with cannot function with the same vitality. The wood element can help. Teaming up with wood people can help them manage their projects and commitments.

Earth People

An earth person's worst fear would be to feel unimportant or not needed. Earth people thrive on fussing over their charges, whether a department team at work or the family unit at home. This is their security. They do not work well independently or enjoy the limelight. The last thing you want to do to is leave earth people alone or separate them from the fold.

Earth people may need to develop more self-esteem and learn to say no. When they are overextended, earth people will no longer feel fulfilled tending to the ones depending on them. They may need to connect with some fire elements. Fire objects (candles, crystals, twinkle lights) often promote optimism and enthusiasm in earth people.

Metal People

One of a metal person's worst fears is a world without rules and guidelines. Metal people spend so much of their lives learning to do what is right socially, politically and morally that they are often worried they could lose control if they try to experience spontaneity or intimacy. They are stressed trying to keep everything on track. At times, even a small change could cause a meltdown.

Metal people need social involvement. Perhaps they could schedule time for different activities outside of work hours. Given a few choices, they may figure out how they can become a little less uptight and more sociable. Warm characteristics and qualities that are present in the earth element can help to warm up and stabilize a metal person's extreme life. A metal person who prefers to stay a loner will find an outlet to satisfy the need for mental stimulation. (Computers, puzzles and games).

Water People

A water person's main fear would be their vulnerability. Water people do not want their privacy invaded. They are very possessive of their ideas, research and accomplishments, and they do not want their identity misrepresented or stolen. Having little or no faith to rely on, they can be extremely pessimistic.

Water people could feel trapped, depressed and anxious while trying to organize their affairs at the same time. They tend to keep pushing themselves without a solid plan until they become road blocked.

I see some water people as lonely, a bit depressed, and unsure of themselves. Referring back to their past, many things have changed, and yet, what is the plan? What is missing is the passion, details and the acceptance to ask for help in the present.

Water people really need the help of all five elements to be well-balanced individuals. If a water person could find room in their life for a spouse or companion, this could be great for adding warmth, trust and balance. Another thing water people need is structure and some boundaries using metal-element qualities. (Metal supports the water element.) More mental stimulation could help them get back on track: games, puzzles, hobbies, music, etc.

The BEST thing about the Five Elements is there's no need to carry these labels throughout your life! There is always room to grow and learn along your journey in life. Recognizing and establishing a dominant element is only a start. Being aware of your weaker elements allows one to improve in these tasks or allow another to take the lead; another win-win!

6   The Cycles of the Five Elements

I love the way these elements continue to teach us about life!

The five elements are arranged in a sequence based on natural elements that can either generate or destroy one another.
—from Living Color: Master Lin Yun's Guide to Feng Shui and the Art of Color

The sequence of the five elements is shown in a circle in the next few diagrams. The arrangement of the five elements shows how they can interact, and this can be used in Feng Shui to balance the strength of physical objects and so much more.

For example: A quick look at one element – fire.

- Earth suppresses fire. If there is a predominance of red in a room (fire), it can be balanced by adding an earth element.
- Wood feeds and supports fire. If the room has a weak fire element, the fire element can be amplified by adding a wood element.
- Water extinguishes fire. Too much of the water element can smother the fire properties in a room.

The example above shows three possible interactions for only one element, fire. To expand on this for all the elements, think of these interactions as cycles within the circle of the five elements. A Feng Shui consultant will work with these elemental cycles when trying to find balance in a room or building.

I believe that when you embrace your dominant personal element, the element cycles can help you function through life's adventures.

We'll look at both tangible items and personalities in this chapter, as we'll use these element cycles to find the balance. The results are fascinating!

There are three cycles I'll discuss: A Productivity & Growth cycle, a Rest & Recovery cycle and an Aggressive Cycle. Each cycle shows a different way the five elements interact, and this can be the *clue* for you to understand how to balance your home and relationships with other people.

Reflections on your personal growth and life experiences will help you further understand the movements of the different cycles. While flourishing in your dominant personal element, you can use this information to seek support from elements on either side—to grow or to rest. The Aggressive Cycle deals with elements that can rub you the wrong way.

Thing about this: The Earth Properties can have existed in perfect harmony for millions of years. They are successfully able to balance fluctuations in growth and change. Imagine!

Wouldn't it be great if we could all embrace our differences and learn to get along?

The Productive and Growth Cycle

This first cycle shows how you can cultivate growth and productivity with support from your adjacent element, clockwise in the circle. I find this cycle fascinating, as well as extremely practical. The productive and growth cycle is just that: productive, progressive and nurturing. This is how one element helps another, in physical form.

- Water nourishes wood (allowing wood to grow).
- Wood feeds the fire (so fire can consume).
- Fire burns out and forms earth (giving earth a foundation).
- Earth (in time) creates metal (giving metal rigidity and strength).
- Metal contains or moves water (giving water flow and purpose).

This cycle becomes an endless loop.

Just as we grow and age, our children grow up and we move from one work environment to another. Smooth associations with people and your environment can change from year to year, season to season, month to month and circumstance to circumstance. We need to adjust and adapt to each new environment, gathering new information and learning new skills along the way.

This is the art of balance. Change, as we grow, is inevitable.

To be well-rounded, we need to adapt regularly.

Five Elements Theory

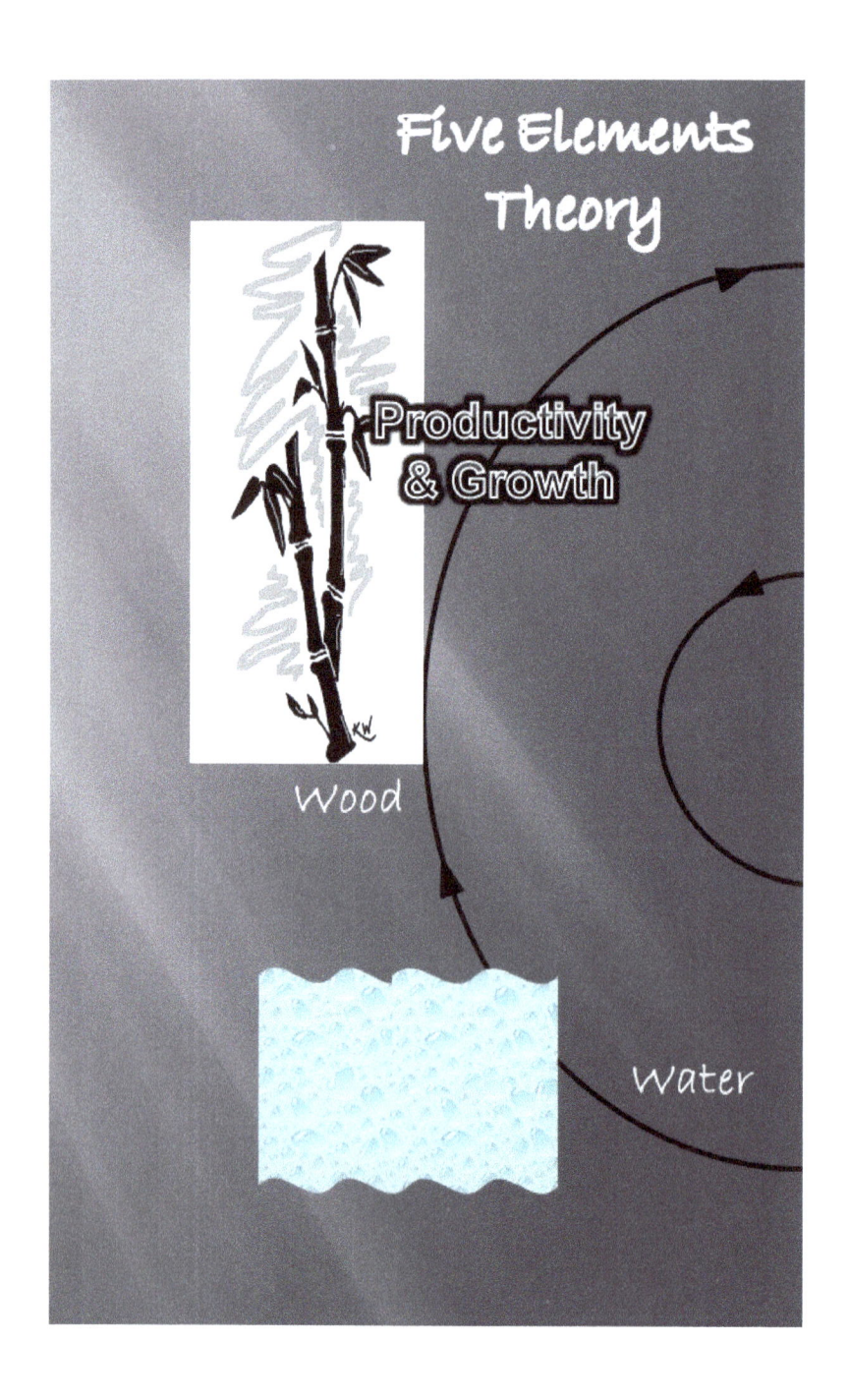

Productivity & Growth

Wood

Water

The Feng Shui Advantage

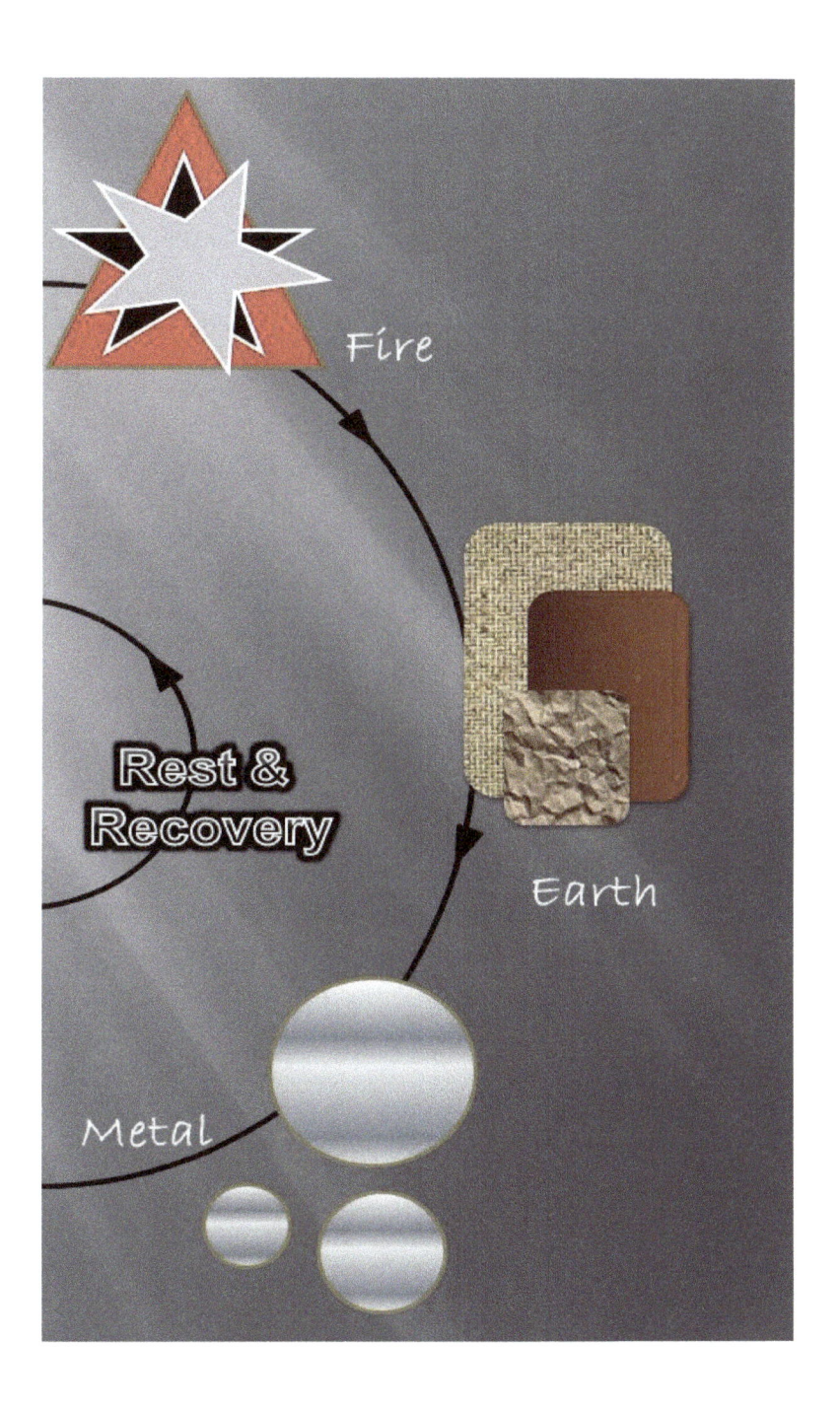

Fire

Earth

Rest & Recovery

Metal

The Recovery Cycle

This section helps you identify the need for rest and recovery, as there will always be a to-do list waiting for you. I really hope that you can take some of the suggestions in this section to heart.

Burnout and exhaustion are often present in today's work scene, no matter how we define it. We all react differently to life's stressors. Try to recognize when you need a break or a timeout and be kind to yourself.

Functioning in your element is fabulous, but you will need a recharging period between peak performances. Rest and recovery are important. People can have different concerns and different setbacks in different situations. We need to learn to adapt. For example, a promotion can lead to another level of politics and challenges that create another level of growth and stress.

In BTB, this cycle is generally referred to as the *reducing cycle*: one element can reduce the effect of the element situated counter clockwise in the cycle. When applying this cycle to people and personalities rather than objects, I prefer to use *recovery* cycle, as I believe this cycle can be adapted as a means to regroup from the stressors in your day and balance the elements that are weak.

Finding the work-life balance takes an open mind to react or regroup with changing times.

Here's how I interpret the recovery cycle:

- Wood growth revitalizes with water. (Wood is nourished with water.)
- Water recharges through metal. (Water becomes charged through metal energy.)
- Metal converts back to earth. (Metal hardness can experience the softness of earth.)

- Earth regenerates through fire. (Earth can be reborn; revives from fire.)
- Fire escalates with wood. (Fire refuels with wood.)

Each element experiences exhaustion and burnout a bit differently and has a different way of recovering.

For example, **wood people**, as busy and organized as they are, can have their fire moments and step up to the plate. But remember, fire can be consuming to wood people. They can burn out easily. In fact, burnout is always pending for true wood people.

When fatigue and despair settle in, wood people first need to get-out-of-the-line-of-fire and then retreat. The best way for wood people to retreat is to get deep into the water element and calm the soul. The water is not only cooler than the fire, it is a place where the wood people can be nourished. Decorating with cool colours and water features can also be calming.

Fire people burn out a little differently than wood people. They tend to consume the energy of those around them and leave the ashes to fall where they may. After reading about fire people earlier in this book, you may recognize people having a fire-moment without being dominant in this element. When fire people tire and need to refuel they require wood people to participate in their projects because they need their wood energy to keep going.

This dramatic tactic gives them the satisfaction of participation, attention and team energy, but not the spotlight. When they have refuelled, they can regroup and get back on the stage.

When **earth people** burn out, they tend to be discreet, unobtrusive and quiet. Generally, the will to keep things the same is both important and stressful for earth people. They avoid change. Being overwhelmed with details can cause them to work harder, and they can easily start acting like metal people—rigid, precise and uncompromising.

By trying to get things right and fix things, they perpetuate more work, and just can't keep it together. A quick fix for earth people who are overcommitted and underappreciated could be to step back and enjoy fire elements. Earth people are drawn to fire: Candles, crystals, twinkle lights, a campfire, etc. They will relax and let someone else take the lead. By regenerating through the fire energy, earth people can set aside their self-appointed deadlines, lighten up and take time to relish the moment.

Metal people are tough ones to read, as they will not allow their emotions to show. They tend to burn out when someone or something has upset their world, such as disorder, fraud and misconduct. Intolerant of any of these issues, they will be burnt out by anxiety. Being unable to sleep or to talk about moral issues can send them into a tailspin.

Metal people who are rallying for a cause need to know when they require support. If they can't get people to listen, their own anxiety could induce an ulcer. A step back into earth-element qualities can be a quiet and comforting break from the rules and regulations of metal world.

The earth element approach will help them calm down. Observing the situation from the sidelines inspires a new strategy to continue. Metal people can consider partaking in a few creature comforts—sip hot apple cider or watch a movie for a change. After taking the time to calm down a bit, they may see how they can redirect their energies.

Quiet and very private, **water people** will never tell you that they are burned out. They are afraid of being exposed. They enjoy being left alone, yet dread being abandoned. A water person who seems unruffled will burn out over something major, such as a political or corporate scandal. Attention and accusations (true or not) would be simply too embarrassing.

When faced with burnout, **water people** must seek support to ward off depression. They can find solace and recharge with the qualities and quiet organized space of the metal element.

Completing crossword puzzles, hobbies, playing cards, watch videos or finding other mental distractions will keep a water person's mind occupied. Water people will function better if they have a support group they can trust to find alternative solutions for their problems.

Use these tips to balance each day! Let's face facts—regardless of the element, whenever you are having a not-so-great-day it is challenging to be productive. Take the time to notice when you are stressed and try to isolate the problem. Then take steps to manage things before you accelerate out of control.

Reader Challenge

Take note of the last time you were overwhelmed working on a project. How did you handle yourself? The situation? Did you manage to fit in some recovery methods? Can you see a pattern forming? A productive pattern? Room for improvement? What are you going to do differently the next time?

Problem identification can often lead to a solution. A few years ago, I hired a virtual assistant, someone opposite to my wood-personality profile. She sorts out the social media needs, marketing, the mailing lists and whatever else I need. Her swiftness and expertise in this area is amazing and so much better than mine! She has freed up time for me to focus on client consultations and my current project of writing this book!

The Cycle of Aggressive Behaviour

We've seen how adjacent elements can nurture others to greater productivity, and also, help with rest and recovery. This third cycle looks at the opposite elements. These are defined by drawing a star pattern inside the circle of the five elements. Those on opposite sides in this cycle can have a detrimental influence on each other, but we still need them. The real challenge is finding a way to work within these parameters.

Our coworkers and family members of our team can all have the same goal, yet find different ways to achieve it. When we get out of our individual comfort zone, we can sometimes rub people the wrong way; and vice versa. When people begin to get stressed, more things start to go wrong and the cycle of aggressive behaviour can be set in motion. Sometimes people just can't see eye to eye.

This cycle is often referred to as the *destructive cycle* or the *restraining cycle* when used by Feng Shui consultants in balancing tangible elements in an environment. The sharp points of the star reveal that these elements can be destructive and penetrating. By using the term *aggressive behaviour* for personality associations, I wish for you to *observe behaviour* between the elements without thinking about your peers as *destructive*. We can find solutions for dealing with different types of people; and, we can all learn to get along.

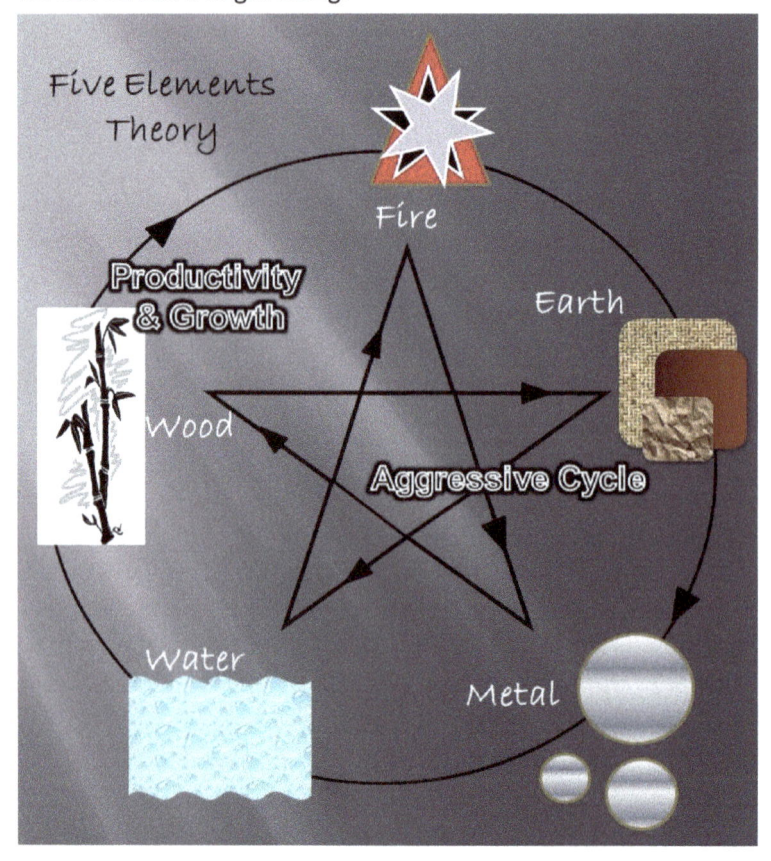

Take a moment to ponder the Aggressive Cycle. These are aggressive words—appropriate when referenced with the sharp, pointed shape of the star. Let's look at the ways aggression makes its way around the cycle, for each of the elements.

- Wood element disrupts earth. (Trees can break through the ground.)
- Earth element dams water. (Earth can actually redirect water.)
- Water element extinguishes fire. (Enough water can drown a fire)
- Fire element melts metal. (Enough fire can re-form metal.)
- Metal element cuts wood. (Sharp metal can chop down trees.)

Now let's see how to read people with the intention of cultivating harmony.

Wood: It is possible for a wood person to devour an earth person. A wood person's aggressive words and over-enthusiasm can overwhelm a calm earth person. The wood person can choose to remain calm when dealing with sensitive earth people, but it is often tough to hold back the excitement, particularly when wood is motivated to go-go-go!

Earth: Though kind-hearted, earth people can stifle water people. Like earth dams up water, it is possible for earth people to confine the movements of water people. Too much coaxing and too much smothering can totally detach and freeze the water person. Be thoughtful, but know when it is best to leave the water person alone. Your co-worker does not want to join in or go to lunch; water people actually *do* accomplish their best work alone.

Fire: For fire people, it is all about *"Me!"* They can melt down the metal people in the Accounting department with ease, maybe just for the fun and excitement. Fire people may get an adrenaline surge when being a bully, but it will be short-lived. They cannot refuel by hanging out with metal people.

Metal: Metal people get tied up in knots when things don't go their way. Their targets are usually wood people because they are the risk-takers. Yes, metal chops wood, and their words are cutting tools. Wood people do require more maintenance in order to, for example, get them to finish their reports or save the receipts! If you want anything completed ahead of time, you may have to—wait for it—*compromise!* Wood people are the ones blazing the trail across the planet, and they have a lot of projects. They will get the job done but not necessarily when you want it.

Water: Knowing that water people are the quietest, it is a bit odd that their favourite target is fire people. In reality, it is easy to understand, because fire people are out there performing and vulnerable. The sting of a water person can literally put out or drown a fire person. It could be a bad review, a mocking tone or a sly sense of humour that humiliates the fame-seeker. Water people need to be aware their humour can be cutting, and perhaps, not funny at all.

Want to neutralize all that aggression? Here are some strategies to try.

- *If you are a wood person,* remember that it is the metal person's job to enforce the rules, keep the books and keep track of everyone and their receipts. Details, details, details. Identify this source of friction between the two of you and then try to cooperate and keep your commitments.

- *If you are an earth person* on the receiving end of a wood person's aggression, offer to support the project or event but otherwise steer clear. You will not be able to keep up with wood people. Be aware that you are only opening yourself up for more criticism, as you cannot do the job fast enough, big enough or strong enough.

- *If you are a water person,* you are dealing with earth people's baggage. They are playing the mother figure, and you are on their mind. "You should come and join us!" they'll say. A polite answer is the best way to handle these requests. Then continue to do what you need to do. No stress and no need to worry.

- *If you are a fire person* and having a bad day, just try to stay away from water people. Seriously.

- *If you are a metal person,* look out for your nemesis, the fire person. An overabundance of a fire element in your corner can lead to a meltdown. Let fire people enjoy their fame while it lasts; no need to participate. Now you know that fire people are all about consumption, keep your head up!

The cycle of aggressive behaviour does exist, although it is often denied. This topic always manages to provoke lively discussions. If you refer back to the chart, you can see that your element can appear to be a bully to another element while a third element bullies you. I know, because I've been there.

I've been accused of being a bully! (What?) And, I've been on the receiving end of a bully. (Really?) It is not always possible to have control when faced with multiple opinions and all its interactions. Decisions need to be made, sometimes at the risk of bruised egos. Be aware of the effects of your actions on other people.

FYI: When evaluating the impact of stressors on a project, the same intensity level can be exhilarating to a wood person, devastating to an earth person and paralyzing to a water person!

> While water and fire are complete opposites, these elements need each other to help maintain control.
> The yin and the yang:
> Water will always represent the low-key force that stores, accumulates and re-stores harmony.
> Fire will always symbolize the high energy of expansion and consumption of energy.

7   Home Harmony

As you learn the patterns of which personal-element-people you get along with, also pay attention to the people on the opposite side of the cycle of aggressive behaviour. They are the ones with a uniquely different set of skills. We have and need diversity in our families and in our teams, to create balance, to foster discussions of new ideas and to delegate various tasks. Recall the dynamics mentioned in the previous chapter.

I was misunderstood growing up; surrounded by metal people in my family. As a dominant wood-person, no one seemed to understand me. I preferred to run through the woods and climb trees than to stay home and study. We all survived, yet these growing years were very harsh for me. Do your kids a favor: recognize their dominant element from the PEP QUIZ so that you can embrace their personality quirks too.

For Home Life: Your 'team' at home includes everyone in the household.

For Businesses: Just as you choose your friends and activities, it is important to choose your team selectively. You will need different people who can fulfil the job description: Sales team, the Marketing team, Accounting, Media, Maintenance, etc. Their education or background may specify one skill or another; yet, are they a good fit in the bigger picture?

When assembling members for a group project, be sure to include diverse personalities. You'll need wood people for the

ideas and leadership, fire people for energy, earth people to supply harmony and a grounded opinion, metal people for accountability and water people for insight, to approve and allow change to happen.

What's Fair?

Some people can sit still for hours, others cannot sit still for five minutes. Know who to delegate each action/task/chore. We all have our own strengths, sometimes through necessity, other times by habit. No one admits to loving chores; but they do need to be done.

I worked in one facility that chose to trim the overhead budget by cancelling the weekly cleaning staff. We were all responsible for cleaning our own office and for pitching in once a week to vacuum the lobby, clean the toilets and empty the trash. I don't really need to give you details about how this turned out—let's just say, some people's standards of *clean* were very different from others. One day, I greeted a client in a less-than-acceptable lobby, I decided that I had to voice my opinion or risk ruining my reputation. I waited for this situation to run its course. Eventually, sanity prevailed, and management rehired the cleaning staff.

In this case, the boss wasn't willing to take cleaning seriously, as his priority was the sales quota. The management needed to hire professional cleaners: end of discussion! Consider an agency to source out extra help whenever help is needed.

Tip: By now, you already know who can push your buttons! If you are hesitating to *ask* someone to take the PEP Quiz, most likely, you can fill in many of the statements yourself by observing other's behavior. The information you have available is simply *how they present themselves to you*, when in your space!

> ### The Family Picnic*
>
> It's usually a **Wood person** that has the idea to plan an event, and gets this in motion.
>
> The **Earth person** will come forward and offer to invite everyone as earth-people have all the phone numbers and contact details.
>
> Next to step up to help will be the **Fire Person**. They are the ones who love to decorate, will organize the music and bring the chocolate cake!
>
> The **Metal Person** will ask "How much is this going to cost?" and "When will it be over?"
>
> The **Water Person** will not commit. There's a 50-50% chance this person will even show up.
>
> *For a successful event, assign the
> right tasks to the right people.

Growing and Changing

As mentioned earlier; when I was learning about these Five Elements and their personalities, I was blown away! I took the PEP Quiz results from my family members and others, and then, applied them to the Five Elements Cycle, and my relationships simply made more sense.

This application can be especially beneficial for raising children. Each child is different. Some are more academically inclined, and others are explorers and need lots of physical activity. Some kids require only one close friend; others need more drama. Let's try to embrace the differences.

As a step-parent, the home life can easily be split into many pieces. Set an example to include everyone, recognize everyone's quirks, interests and talents. Make sure everyone gets a voice,

and a chair, so everyone can learn to thrive in this crazy world. I counsel parents about embracing their children's unique differences, rather than label and ridicule their interests.

Your team and family members need to develop clear goals and coordinate with each other. Be clear about the changes and expectations in the next month or year. The more visuals, confirmations and information you display to reinforce what is expected, the more everyone is onboard, moving and working together.

In order to make a change in your work responsibilities or your life goals, something has to shift. Sometimes, it is as easy as reframing things and setting very clear goals. Any new chi energy has a domino effect and will be noticed by others, allowing you to be productive and live life to the fullest.

Use the word 'team' and you'll develop a team mentality; working together. Whether it be your family or coworkers, give your team the tools they need to succeed!

The Royal WE

It is easy to fall into a routine when we are confident and comfortable with our day to day activities. Occasionally, we can get frustrated and fretful with our routine, pointing fingers and accusations. We're going to shift this energy by using selective words to bring everyone back together. Let's face it, we all want to feel important. We all want to belong.

The tasks and projects handed down from a boss, mom or person-in-charge need the 'royal we' in order to work together –for the common good of all.

Reframing your language into something more supportive may be another tool for you!

Altering your vocabulary to include the 'Royal WE' can go a long way. You can still maintain control in a harmonious way, without blame or disrespect. Start by using the words 'we' or 'let's. This will remind other about their place in the family, your team, each other; see if magic happens in your space.

Instead of situations like these:

- "It is your turn to take out the garbage."
- "I'm busy tonight, I have to shop for groceries."
- "Why did you buy this cereal? You know it has too much sugar in it!"

Reframe these statements and insert the 'Royal WE' to diffuse any issues; turn the issue into a statement, rather than blaming or complaining.

Some suggestions:

- "We need to get the garbage out this evening. Who's turn is it this week?"
- "We are all busy tonight, yet, we still need groceries. Who's coming with me?"
- "We need to remember not to buy this type of cereal, it's full of sugar."
- "We need to address this issue tomorrow. Let's try to find a solution."
- "Let's figure out how to clean this up quickly, together."
- "Thanks for the group effort this week; we sorted out the problem together. Let's all learn from this."

For me personally, I found this technique taught me a lot about patience when dealing with both my husband and children. It is a great way to be more diplomatic, rather than critical.

Try using the 'Royal WE' when working with your corporate team. It works to help build trust and inclusiveness.

Do you need to find harmony during a hectic day?

The 'Royal WE' is also a great peace keeper.

Let's do this together!

~

8   Finding the Wealth

Luck, fortune and abundance can be found in many forms.

When people ask me about Wealth and Abundance, I turn the question back to them: What do you think about wealth? What are you looking for? Wealth can be measured in acquisitions: a strong portfolio, real estate and bank accounts. Abundance can show up in the form of many grandchildren, magnificent flowers or a litter of kittens.

How we deal with money and wealth can usually be traced back to the attitudes formed by our parents and *their* approach to money. Many of these early experiences with money are based on past economics times and limited information at that time. We often need to look at these imprinted barriers, restrictions and fears, instilled by others. These hidden barriers often determine our self-worth; keeping us from achieving what we want. Overcoming the restrictions in-our-head is the key to our earnings and successes.

Feng Shui speaks of Wealth in terms of luck, fortune and abundance. We need to define what we are seeking in order to find to look for. This chapter will guide you into a fresh mindset and new awareness to cultivate abundance in all your actions!

Let's get set up for cultivating Wealth and Abundance!

Where do I find wealth in my world? Is it just floating around in the sky?

> *Each of us is a millionaire.*
> *It is hidden beneath years of programming from our parents,*
> *our ancestors and our society at large.*
> —Sonia Haynes, *The Power of Money*

Positive thinking is the first step to setting clear boundaries for your goals and what you wish to achieve. This is a starting point to setting 'cures and enhancements' for the things you desire. Positive thinking will help 'make the shift' in many areas, creating a ripple effect.

In order for you to receive abundance and wealth, you first need clear intentions. These should be envisioned with purpose, gratitude and goodwill. Have a plan, be open for expansion!

I challenge my clients and podcast listeners to **better themselves** 1% each day. Just 1%! In fact, if that is too much to imagine, start small. Shift your mind by 1% each week! If we all made an effort each day to better ourselves even 1%, we'd feel better and BE better. You'll have more energy, more focus and when properly rested, you'll be able to make sound decisions and help others. It's a WIN-WIN!

When you raise the vibration for yourself, you'll raise the vibration in the environment around you too! Your insight will be a new tool for life! You, and only you, can decide which issues to address *inside* in order to move forwards.

Your words will also influence the energy vibration in self, people around you and the environment. Successful people use passionate adjectives when talking about wealth. Words like *fortunate, good luck, auspicious, promising, prosperous* and *favourable* are often used in decisive reasoning. With practice, successful people will place an intention, and take action, in key areas of their lives where they desire opportunities, enhancements and reinforcements.

In contrast, if you are complaining or criticizing others, this becomes a lower vibration. Lower vibrations make the mood heavy; it can be difficult to pull the energy back up. Stick with the lighter, more positive, encouraging vibrations and you'll see how much more you can achieve!

Supports for positive intentions require cleaning; a deep clean in all areas. You need to cull/purge/remove/gift/toss or shift any tangible items and their energy around you to make change. You've heard this before: Clean your space and clear out the clutter to **make room for more.** Surround yourself with ONLY the things that you love and will support your intentions.

Select the items you want to keep in this new energetic space. Clean and reorganize these items with good intentions to keep the 'new space' special. The *action* of cleaning is such a simple and practical way for you to **take control;** in your Wealth Area or another area of life. This cleaning-up is a positive action to sift out what you really need and really want!

Each room, whether it be your office, the dining room or the bedroom, will come with its own challenges to find what makes sense. For an expanded version of cures and enhancements check out The Expanded Bagua in Appendix B.

With a solid attitude and a solid plan, any nay-sayers will not have any influence over your goals. Be firm with what feels best for you.

Personal Expression
Dress codes have changed over the past few years.

Your choice of clothing gives others a clue about what mood you are in and how you plan to proceed. If you are confident, clothing can help you send that message. I am not talking about brand names, lipstick and bling, although some people feel they need these items. The colours you choose to wear can reflect the way you feel about yourself professionally and have an impact on others in business. I'm suggesting that you make an effort to *present yourself in the way you wish to be seen.*

In the corporate world, there is an image that we need to uphold. In every company and every division, there are nuances. Sending the right message is extremely important when you are doing business whether you are an owner or a client. Dress in a way that represents you confidently; you'll receive better service and respect wherever you go.

How do you wish to present yourself today?

We already talked a bit about ZOOM, Skype or other video platforms, you need to present yourself positively. Your professional calls should reflect that you are in business, and also, you are worthy of getting paid. Personal calls can allow a more casual appearance. Respect your audience, take the time to clean up, comb your hair and put on something appropriate. For more information about ZOOM calls, see Chapter 1.

Setting a positive tone for the day can be done with your wardrobe.

- If you are dealing with issues involving insurance, investments or technology, calm colours can quiet the mind and help you pay attention. You may find that wearing darker, sober colours promote trust and insight.
- If you wish to increase your productivity, choose a bright-coloured tie, scarf or outfit. This will get people to notice you, keeping you on your toes while making new contacts.
- If you are trying to stimulate your mind, try wearing something blue, red or purple. These colours reflect inspiration, royalty and higher ground.
- Utilize the colour green or blue; these colours represent growth and possibilities.
- If you are stuck in a dull grey city for an entire winter, try wearing bright colours. Fresh, inspiring colours can be uplifting on a particularly bleak day.

A fresh colour in your wardrobe could help to raise your vibration! Keep those brain synapses firing!

Enhancements

A Feng Shui crystal is round and multifaceted; numerous light refraction areas will bring rainbows into your space, all year round!

Think of enhancements as attention-getters. Feng Shui presents you with an assortment of choices that can bring attention to your space and help to reinforce intentions. The intention is not to turn your space into a Chinese Circus! Choose only the ones that make sense to you in each space.

- *Lights:* Good lighting, mirrors and light-refracting objects gather energy and move it around. Crystal balls, vases or jewellery work well too. Place your mirrors where they can bring in more light and reflect something pleasant to look at.
- *Sounds:* Softer, pleasant sounds are far better for concentration and productivity. White noise can block out unwanted distractions. Wind chimes or

bells hung near an entrance can announce a customer or alternately, an intruder.
- *Colours:* Choose items that are bright-coloured: neon pink-orange, purple and red. The intention would be to attract attention towards a product, your business achievements or yourself.
- *Life:* Plants that are blooming, have berries, or are red in colour are great enhancements and draw attention. Living, healthy plants are preferred, yet not always appropriate. You can bring in a quality representation of a plant to use for an enhancement. Any orchid, flowers or fish that you choose, real or man-made, make great enhancements.
- *Children and Pets:* The life energy of these happy additions, do enhance our lives. Displaying happy moments as they grow and change are also recommended. But keep these photos out of the master bedroom. (Only room for two people.)
- *Moving Objects:* Wind-powered or electrically powered mobiles or whirligigs can also be classed as enhancements. They stimulate circulation in a stale area. Any movement from moving objects can awaken the monotony of a long corridor.
- *Heavy Objects:* A heavy stone or statue can help you stay grounded. If you are trying to secure a project, deal with a situation or just be more focused, a large rock or clay pots properly placed, can stabilize the situation.

Reader's Challenge: Take a look at your space. You may be surprised which enhancements are already working for you!

"What would the world be like without any enhancements?"
~ my friend, Marjory Schurman

Choose an image that inspires you to be your best!

Career and Wealth Areas

Water represents *money*! Physical water can be seen in the form of fountains, aquariums, bowls, ponds and vases. But water can also be represented by the colour blue, a wavy pattern or a picture with healthy, clean water. Tumbled stones can also represent water or a water feature.

Water is the element associated with the *Career Area*. And, since water nourishes wood, the *Family Area* and *Wealth Area* can benefit also. In business, these water features are intended to create activity, inspire positive energy and encourage forward-thinking looking into the future.

If you choose to use real water in your enhancement, be sure the water is consistently clean and clear. If you'd like to add fish or plants into your space, keep them healthy. For the exact number of fish or plants, you can either choose the number designated to the 'area of life' you wish to enhance or choose another auspicious number to act as a reinforcement.

Tip: The number nine is auspicious in Feng Shui; the highest single digit of all! If your space will not accommodate 'nine of anything', reduce this number to three. A 'small nine' will work just fine!

If your plumbing pipes run in an area that you are trying to enhance, you need to watch for water—also representing money—running down the drain. Too much water can signify a potential loss of resources. Go back to the basics. Keep the bathroom door closed and the toilet lid down if it is near your office or entrance.

If you are shopping for a water fountain for a desk or reception area, size *does* matter. Be sure to scale a water feature to the space available. (With every 'cure', consider the magnitude of space allowed.) A feature for a desk should be considerably smaller than one you choose for an entrance or the garden.

Entrance

The entrance and doorway into your office or cubicle is very significant. The main opening is related to the mouth of the structure, business and operations. If this mouth is blocked in any way, the energy—chi—will be stagnant. With an energy block in these areas, you could have issues with productivity, production, and prosperity.

Greet yourself daily with things that are calming and cheerful: a welcoming painting, colourful flowers and a small table to catch your keys and packages. A crystal chandelier can grace your welcome area by sending little bits of light and energy into all the corners. A solid welcome mat is both grounding and welcoming.

The mat should be a dark blue or black colour, as this relates to your career security and your interaction with the outside world.

By keeping the entrance clean, clear and accessible, you should be able to cultivate new opportunities to your door. Stay positive and look for opportunities coming into your space.

Readers Challenge:

Have a new look at your entrance to the workspace (wherever that may be) with fresh eyes. Is it fabulous? Is your office or workspace pulling you back or pushing you towards success.

Where Is the Wealth?

Your personal definition of wealth and abundance may be very different from another person's. Success can be registered in many ways and materialize in many forms. Many people seek fulfillment in their positions through the money they earn, others seek job satisfaction in services. You may recall, the Wealth Area is located in the upper left area of the floorplan. For a 'cheat sheet' of enhancement for each area, refer to the Expanded Bagua in Appendix B.

I suggest you be specific and write down your goals, if you haven't done this already. It is time to set your goals in motion. They can be decadent and even unrealistic. They can be tangible or not. They can be anything you want, just be specific. Be sure to date the piece of paper and put it in a safe place: in your desk, under a coaster or taped to the back of a picture frame in your wealth area. You should review the list at the end of the year/expired time. You may want to refer to it and make adjustments for future goals.

> In order to *manifest a serious shift* in your life, you will need to raise your vibrational energy in order to make it happen.

Your Big Goals – What do you want?

The energy of the Five Elements will strengthen each area of your office and your life. There is no need to go out and spend a lot of money; you have auspicious elements in your home and office right now. Gather the five elements together by using colour, shapes or anything in your imagination. Whatever you choose is very personal and needs to resonate within yourself.

I am a firm believer in the power of visual enhancements as mentioned in Chapter 3. Everyday items can reinforce your goal, keeping them 'front and centre':

- A picture or postcard can have the colours and locations where you want to go.
- A scarf can feature all the shapes and the textures to inspire your desires.
- A coffee cup can feature an inspiration for the day ahead.
- A glass bowl of coloured stones and a candle can help your dream.

Scale up your enhancements to your goals, wants, dreams and desires. Larger goals require larger enhancements. You may want to focus on a specific area in your office. Remember, the wealth area is located in the far-left corner of your room, building or property.

One easy enhancement is to add plants to your space; as long as they are healthy, living, breathing and growing! You may utilize quality silk flowers if maintenance and good lighting is an issue.

Bamboo is a symbol of good fortune, good health and prosperity. This plant attracts and increases the flow of positive energy placed anywhere in your office or home. Other auspicious house plants to use: orchids, jade plant, peace lily, snake plant, money tree. In fact, any plant that is healthy and hearty will bring joy and life in to a space; a bonus if they are flowering!

> Please do not bring dead plants into your space. They are dead; no energy. Take a picture of the momentous occasion or flowers and discard when the flowers are past their prime. This rule includes, pot pourri, wreaths, dried grasses twigs and the like.

Attract richness to your wealth area, by displaying tangible things of value to you: antique rugs or furniture, pearls or gems, coins, crystal or carvings. Pictures with a representation of wealth, such as fishing trips or vacations to exotic location are also great in this area. These choices are very personal. I can't tell you specifically what to place in this area for enhancement for your goals. I can only make suggestions for you to consider. Perhaps you are more comfortable displaying a picture of your hard-earned rewards: a sailboat, vacation home or unusual purchase. I'm sure you have plenty of remarkable items to choose from.

To make this area more auspicious and to gather more attention, add a large mirror to magnify the wealth. If your goal is cold hard cash, you may want to add a cache of antique coins to your display. I've also seen fine jewellery hung from a lamp or a vase to reinforce a wealth area.

In some enthusiastic cases, people place real paper money into a display on a buffet or end table. A note to cash enthusiasts: Apply a little caution when displaying cash in your home. Some visitors may view this as flaunting or tempting, as a client of mine found out!

Now that I have you excited about raising the vibration for cultivating wealth and abundance in your home, let's go back to the goals and intentions for action.

What is the purpose of 'more'? What are you saving for? Good intentions will always carry a higher vibration.
So, what excites you?

Are these wishes just a dream? Will these accomplishments enhance your lifestyle? Can they also benefit others? How can you embrace these goals into an action plan?

I'm all for **visuals** for the BIG GOALS in life! View them on walls, closet doors, desktop, the frig and anywhere else!

So, what's your goal?

Drive a classic car?

Own your dream home?

Kathryn Wilking

Experience a sunrise in Grand Cayman Island?

Post Graduate Education?

Or, Just Sail Away from it all?

Visit your wealth area often; every few weeks to keep things clutter-free and fresh. If you are living/working in a private space, you can make these enhancements without having to answer to anyone.

Author's Personal Results Regarding the Wealth Area

When I asked my husband the question, "Would it be a problem for you if I enhanced our wealth area?", he was open for change, as long as I promised not to do anything too weird. What we didn't discuss was the definition of weird!

Our wealth area on the main floor was in the dining room. Dining rooms are easy to enhance, as they often already have a dining area, fancy dishes and linens. In our case, the enhancement items chosen were antique rugs, tall plants and floor-to-ceiling draperies. My personal choice for the focal point was two, tall hand-carved ebony giraffes that we bought in Africa. They not only represented a once-in-a-lifetime trip, but they are both stunning and exotic for representation in the wealth area.

Early on in my Feng Shui lessons, I arranged some enhancements in our house with the intention to increase the cash flow. What happened next was a promotion for Stephen, a free gym membership and I won a year's supply of bread from the local Cobb's bakery! Yep, 52 loaves of bread!

Be careful what you wish for...

Over the past 20 years, using Feng Shui theories and principles, I can honestly say that our lives have been greatly enhanced; more function, order and less stress.
Feng shui has allowed us grow and prosper:
- buying and selling properties
- making sound investments
- cultivating help when needed
- form solid relationships
- setting a positive vibration for a full happy lifestyle

Feng Shui is practical, ethical and it never goes out of style!

Real Snapshots

My client Susan had placed new, real, paper money tucked in under the runner of her sideboard table in the dining room; all $50. bills. She checked on it periodically, encouraging it to work for her. When spring cleaning, she found three of the bills had been used. Used? The only way brand-new bills can be used is if someone borrowed the money and then replaced it. Whoever borrowed the money did not pay attention to fact that the originals were brand new bills! The mystery remains unsolved. At least she got paid back. A word of caution...

Ellen and Ryan set up a lovely antique chess set in their wealth area. They made a stunning display in the display cabinet in their dining room with a set of red and green place mats and brass treasures. They also placed a case of poker chips at the base of the cabinet. Their interpretation of the wealth area was that they were gambling and hoping to cash in on the high stakes sometime soon. Last time I talked with the couple, their investments were doing just fine. Optimism is key to look for opportunities!

Anna asked me for help after her husband died. She wanted to sell the house but was waiting for the housing market to bounce back. Could I help cheer up the house a little to keep its value from slipping? Her wealth area was the living room, predominantly black, cream and white. Anna initially resisted my attempts to bring in more colour, but I did manage to move some blue pots over to the fireplace hearth to soften their huge 2-story fireplace.

We went through her wardrobe to search for her favourite colours and selected one of her fine silk scarves to drape over the baby grand piano and added a cute lamp. The scarf and the lamp brought a nice softness to the piano area.

Lastly, I found her grandchild's little teddy bear in a basket of toys and placed it on the couch. The teddy bear was wearing a little red sweater that read "Home Sweet Home." Anna was delighted! She feels much better in her home. She can now enjoy her house while waiting for the right time to sell.

James, a department manager, was a little frustrated with his career when I met him. The corporation was reshuffling again, and he was afraid that this was the last rung on the ladder for him. After his wife and I worked through a few enhancements at their home, I went to his office in a corporate tower to evaluate his desk and work area. I asked James to draw a picture of an aquarium on the whiteboard near his desk, with 24 black fish and 3 red fish.

A month later, James received the promotion he deserved, with a nice raise! This fortune was already in motion when I met him. The enhancements gave him the attention and focus needed for his promotion to come through. I asked him a few weeks later if the fish were still on his whiteboard, and he replied, "Oh yes, no one has noticed." But, I think someone did!

Sue, a depressed water person, decided to move her antique piano and imported rugs into her wealth area located in the spare bedroom. A few months later, she was disappointed, as she expected her bank account would suddenly double in size. When I followed up with Sue, I explained to her that she needed to *open the door* to the bedroom, let in fresh chi energy and perhaps *play* the piano. She needed to *enhance the enhancements* in order to keep them from becoming stagnant and stale. Sue also agreed that it was time to work on other areas; helpful-people and health. She needs to be in a better frame of mind to recognize and enjoy any wealth opportunities when they do arrive on her doorstep.

By putting attention and focus into your wealth area, you will be more focused on your intention to earn money, spend wisely or rediscover assets that you may have forgotten. Search through your life and imagine a way to manifest your greatest desires.

When we learn to look at things differently, we open up new definitions of what wealth means to each of us.

Woo-Woo? Weird stuff we can't see...

The main intention of this section is to encourage you to look at things differently. And then use this opportunity to take charge of your own space, your stuff and your life!

We started this book with the First Layer of Feng Shui; learning about function and flow though the Power Position. We followed that with the Second Layer, about the supportive messages we send ourselves though colors, shapes and images. The Third Layer is the spiritual or metaphysical component; what I refer to as the 'woo-woo'. (The weird stuff we cannot see).

Feng Shui definitely includes 'things you cannot see'.

Many Feng Shui experts combine several metaphysical ideas into their services. Anything from ergonomics, safety issues, numerology, face reading, dowsing, pendulum, space clearing, singing bells, scented oils, meditation, blessing rituals and more. When you are 'in tune' with the energy of yourself, your space and your environment, you'll *know* you are in the groove of something wonderful! This is where you set intention and make things change! Chi-energy at it's BEST!

Most Alternate-care practitioners have their own specific routine each day to help *connect to a higher force.* By doing so, they raise their own vibrational energy, in order to help others. There are many emerging services and a lot of information to sift through to discover what may work best for you. You'll figure it out.

*Surround yourself with only things, and people,
that bring joy and love into your life!*

Get yourself ready to embrace life to the fullest:

Set yourself up for success: Only a true connection begins when you stop moving.

Be quiet. It is so difficult these days to slow down and be still. Ground yourself.

Listen to the stillness. Slow down your breathing.

Tune in to your heart beat, if you need to. Relax.

Acknowledge that there is a higher power. Connect to your *higher power*; in whatever *name* that may resonate for you.

Turn off the mind-chatter. Only then, can you think positive thoughts and make sound decisions for positive change in your life; whatever that may be.

Feng Shui promotes clean, healthy positive living -what we all need more of these days. Ask forgiveness. Be grateful. Feel compassion for fellow humans, animals, trees, mother earth and more.

There's a Hawaiian meditation that you can use while walking, resting, driving and everywhere else. It's called **Ho'oponopono**. It includes the most powerful, compassionate statements you can speak in life:

I love You. Thank You. Forgive Me. I'm sorry.

Repeat as often as you desire in any situation. This is so easy to work into your day; it covers all the bases and topics in life. I love the repetition.

Creating new habits takes time. Learning quiet and patience is also a new skill. Be kind to yourself. Embrace what works for you, and leave the rest for now. Magic just doesn't happen on a whim; we need to recognize that a consistent, positive effort is required on our part.

9   Making the Shift

No matter what is going on in your life right now, I can guarantee it will not last forever. Good or not-so-good.

Things and people come and go. Children grow up. We get older. Everything shifts. Our journey continues to move forwards taking us through all the stages and phases of life.

We can choose resistance when having to make change, or we can embrace the challenges as another learning experience.

Embrace each day as unique and wonder; what's going to happen today? Be flexible. Does our home have to look like a polished magazine photo every day? Of course not. Life is for the living. Have fun. Set boundaries. Relax a bit and take charge whenever you can. Enjoy time with your spouse and family.

Before you know it, there will be more changes on the horizon.

Reader Challenge

I challenge you all to take the first step – begin to look at things a bit differently in your life. You can find abundance in your life that you never knew you had.

When applying your Feng Shui enhancements, write down the date and the specifics of how and why you selected the enhancements to make change. Observe how the energy patterns shift when you are committed. Embrace the woo-woo.

I welcome your comments and questions; I'm curious to know how you are maneuvering on your journey through life. I look forward to hearing from you!

Let me know how I can help you further.

Together, we can make the world a better place to live and thrive!

It's been my honor and pleasure to share these tips, secrets and insight with you today. May you find, and keep, the balance in your life!

Kathryn Wilking.com https.www.kathrynwilking.com
E-mail: kathryn@kathrynwilking.com

Podcast: **Feng Shui Your Day** on Spotify, Apple, I Heart and more.
Podcast: **Good Vibes Change Lives** on You Tube, Spotify, Apple, I Heart and more.

Appendix A: More about the Power Position

The Power Position (AKA: Command Position) refers back to a Chinese model from the fourth century BC when people were searching for the best place to bury their ancestors. The logic goes as follows:

- *The back of the Command Position* is represented by the image of a **tortoise**. The back, which is blind to us personally, is extremely vulnerable. You'll need to have your back protected. This will lower anxiety on the subconscious level.

- *The front of the Command Position* is represented by the image of the **phoenix**, a bird of perpetual inspiration. Your eyes need to see a clear, unobstructed view. You want to see all that is going on in the room and environment. You'll be more inspired when you are able to see a broad panorama looking into the future.

- *Your right side* is represented by the **tiger** and possesses great strength, yet, also requires control and restraint. Energies and objects on your right side will need to be closer to the ground, representing a tamed wildcat ready to move. A small table, such as an end table with enhancements, is a great solution.

- *The left side* is represented by the **dragon**. The dragon is far-sighted and very wise. This animal represents a calm, open mind symbolizing our desire to have a broad outlook on life. The dragon can rise above ordinary eye levels, which is why you are advised to place taller items here, on the left side.

These ideas can be implemented and relevant in today's world when assessing working and living areas. You can use this model in very practical ways to assess the psychological impact of furniture and the *best spot* in a room when you eat, sleep and work. Be aware of your surroundings and establish secure locations wherever meeting people and social settings.

Check out all your positions in your life to see if you are in charge of your power position: sitting at your desk, while you eat, sleeping in the right place, relaxing after work, in the restaurant, the coffee shop or a waiting room. Can you feel the difference after shifting the energy in these areas?

Appendix B: The Expanded Bagua

The bagua, as stated earlier, can have many interpretations in Feng Shui. This appendix gives you only five (of the many) interpretations for each gua. This is plenty of information to get you moving toward your goals.

The Life Designations

The Knowledge, Career and Helpful-people Areas are situated the closest to the entrance. They are the *guas* that are interactive with your daily activities and depend on situations outside the confines of your home or office to provide fulfilment, education and help.

The Family, Health and Children Areas are situated in the center. They are representative of your body and health and extend to your offspring and heritage lines. These are simple facts—who you are and where you are from.

The Wealth, Fame and Relationship Areas are very private and very personal. It is appropriate they are positioned far away from the entrance to the rest of the world. This is where your personal soul and the private, delicate intimacies in life are kept.

The numbers in the bagua grid are auspicious to their own life areas. Numerology has its own school and has multiple levels of interpretation. Try to utilize the numbers in each area while arranging plants, flowers, pictures and more in the areas you want to enhance.

The Bagua:
Nine Areas of Life and their Elements.

WEALTH AND ABUNDANCE	FAME	RELATIONSHIPS
• Represents: Wealth and prosperity • Shape: Tall, columns • Colours: Purple, red, green • Element: Wood • Number: 4	• Represents: Reputation and achievements • Shape: Triangle, sharp things • Colours: Red • Element: Fire • Number: 9	• Represents: Love, marriage and partnerships • Shape: Squares and rectangles • Colours: Red, pink • Element: Earth • Number: 2
FAMILY	**HEALTH**	**CHILDREN & CREATIVITY**
• Represents: Ancestor line and belonging • Shape: Tall, columns • Colours: Green • Element: Wood • Number: 3	• Represents: Everything • Colours: Yellow and earth tones • Element: Earth • Number: 5	• Represents: Creative influences • Shape: Oval, round • Colours: Grey, white, metallic • Element: Metal • Number: 7
KNOWLEDGE AND WISDOM	**CAREER AND LIFE PATH**	**HELPFUL PEOPLE AND TRAVEL**
• Represents: Knowing and self cultivation • Shape: Square and rectangle • Colours: Earth tones • Element: Earth • Number: 8	• Represents: Life's path • Shape: Wavy • Colours: Black, dark blues • Element: Water • Number: 1	• Represents: Helpful exchange, benefactors • Shape: Oval, round • Colours: Grey, white, metallic • Element: Metal • Number: 6

Line up your desk, doorway or entrance with this edge.

Property of Kathryn Wilking Designs; prepared for the purpose of bringing balance and harmony to people's lives. www.kathrynwilking.com

Floor Plans

If you have a large area to assess, it will be easier to comprehend if you lay out the bagua grid on a floor plan. Many floor plans are somewhat irregular, so here is how to proceed:

- First, line up the bagua grid with the entrance or main doorway as previously shown.
- Line up the side edges of the bagua, one side at a time.
- If an outside or inside wall is irregular, determine which wall is the longest and use that to place the edge of the bagua in line with the wall.
- The bagua grid is flexible and can be layered. Draw the interior bagua lines. Evenly space three squares wide and three squares long within the floor plan, and then again for each room to see the layers. You may find a wealth area *inside* another wealth area! Double Wealth enhancements!

There will be areas of the floor plan that fall outside of your bagua and areas within the bagua that the floor plan doesn't cover. These are your bonus and missing spaces. If you have space outside of the bagua configuration, this is great news! This is a bonus for whatever section of the bagua it's attached to. Take advantage of this by using auspicious enhancements and keep working for you. For spaces that appear to be 'missing' within the bagua grid, there are 'cures' to square-off the area or from your floor plan.

As all 'cures' are individual, please consider the notes in this book before winging it. If you have other issues or do not know where to start, please contact a certified Feng Shui professional regarding how to match your 'cure' with your goals in life.

Appendix C: EMF's and You!
(Electromagnetic Frequencies)

I had to include in this topic in this Appendix. I've been passionate for 10 years watching, reading and searching for the answers to keep us all safe from radiation frequencies.

While I've uncovered a lot of scary data about the pulses of our multi-device lifestyles, and embrace the cautionary tales of use, there's still *so much* we don't know about the effects of these pulses on our human body.

While we've been dealing with the depleting Ozone Layer, global warming, and political issues abroad, the technology in our modern world has been evolving. As a result, we spend our daily lives in fields of low and high frequency electro-magnetic radiation: EMF's.

Our everyday technology now includes a plethora of cell phones, computers and assorted wireless devices. As efficient as they may be, they also produce overlapping fields of radiation permeating throughout our modern world.

Until the twentieth century, the greatest emitter of electro-magnetic radiation was the sun! We now know about UVA and UVB rays, and understand the importance of a good sunscreen, but there are more risks we need to be aware of.

The World Health Organization stated back in 2012: "We believe that Electro-Magnetic Fields will be one of the greatest environmental health challenges for the coming generations."

That was more than ten years ago! So, what are we supposed to do?

Mobile phone use has evolved from an uncommon activity about 25 years ago, to one with over billions of users worldwide. With our dependence on these items in today's society, there is public concern about the possibility that mobile phones might cause cancer, especially brain tumours. The studies that follow this data are still in discussion because the information doesn't date back farther than 20 years.

Regardless of when the data will be completed, we know that some of this new technology is already affecting some of the population. **One of the most common diseases of the 21st century is stress.** As we learn to live with stressors, our immune system *is* affected; this is the time when EFMs will affect us the most. Yes, there is proof that the frequent pulses of EMF'S in 'developing brains' of children and teens are more susceptible than adults, but to what degree?

I own an Energy Frequency Monitor, for use in my services. One misunderstanding is how to register these pulses for exposure. A low number/value of this pulse can appear to be safe. But the issue is the 'LENGTH OF TIME' you are exposed to this environment. So take a look at the places that you sit/sleep/work the most, which will influence your total exposure in a day.

I often visit clients who have an octopus of cords beside their favorite chair! While the EMF's can test 'within normal parameters', long term exposure can weaken immune systems; especially for the very young and very old.

A few things you can do to minimize your exposure to EMF's:

CELL PHONES and Bluetooth Use the speaker phone option or texting your messages are safer options. The battery is usually in the back, so if you can, carry your phone battery facing away from your body. Be sure to charge your cell phone away from your body and away from your bed when not required.

Again, the data is still being evaluated as to how much harm these portable mini-waves can affect us. If we have to be carful of the radiation pulse of a cellphone, what about Bluetooth ear pieces which plug right into your head?! You evaluate what is best for you and your kids.

CORDLESS PHONES and Lamps   Transformers for these items send out high energy pulses constantly, day and night, regardless of usage or not. The transformer that comes with each unit measures 'within normal range' on an EMF scale, but still be aware. If these transformers are in your home, place the charging units away from your favourite sitting areas and bedside by at least three feet or 1 meter. They emit radiation **continuously,** so that the overall EMF levels can be significantly higher than cellphones. Few people are aware of this. Ideally, a reliable, safe phone at home should be a corded phone.

MODEMS   Use an Ethernet cable for your modem if possible for a direct connection. If you have a wireless modem, choose one which easily can be shut off at night with just a simple button. By actually shutting things down, the item will not emit EMF's all night in your house or affect your body's sleep rhythms.

COMPUTERS   A laptop computer often has the battery in the back, so front exposure is less for the primary user. Yet, when you are coordinating and sharing space with others, your battery is facing your friends/family. If used on your lap, the experts suggest that you use a board, tray or blanket underneath to displace the energies.

EMF' can walk through walls, and, this happens at all frequency ranges. The same EMF emissions from your cell phone also run through the power lines in the wall behind a bed or under the desk. Our bodies are as sensitive to these emissions; if you are sharing a wall with another room- condo-office, you many consider 'protective devices' to defer exposure. Alternative and reputable contacts for EMF Protection are listed in the Resources below.

Take frequent breaks from your work station if possible.

BEDROOM   A TV continues to emit EMF's after you turn it off. Keep any music players and electronic games away from you and your children's beds while sleeping. A full nights sleep = an 8-hour exposure!

Please shut off or remove tablets from the night table.

True Case Story: I was at a client's home a few years ago. The gentleman was newly retired and starting a small business transferring digital things: 8 track tapes to disc and vinyl records (LP's) to digital. I expected a major SURGE in this room, but, with his updated equipment the readings on my meter were quite low. The item that tested the highest in his office was a battery driven radio/alarm clock from the 70's. Hmm...

True Case Story: Another client of mine confidentially told me that her husband sleeps with his cell phone charging on his chest! Really?
As I got into his mind-space, I could sort-of see his logic. As an owner of a construction company, he would need to be notified asap if anything shifted or changed that would need a decision at anytime of the night and day. Yet, the angst that he'd miss-a-call was causing his wife to wonder if his heart will stop one day? His behavior was doing more damage to the relationship exposing his wife to these emissions, interfering with *her* sleep and their intimate time together.

My suggestion to the husband in this story and any others that really NEED to see their phones first-thing-in-the-morning: set up a charging station in the washroom. That's exactly where everyone heads to first thing in the morning. The husband did place his phone in the washroom for two nights, and then, decided to go back to sleeping with the phone on his chest. Oh well...his choice.

The more we are aware, the better choices we can make for our home and families. Some of these issues listed may appear to be insignificant or even petty to address, however, today is only one day out of our lives absorbing Electromagnetic Radiation. If we are planning to live out a full life span, radiation overexposure CAN and WILL disrupt your cells. We should be cutting down on our radiation exposure in any way possible.

> What you can do NOW is be aware, play safe, and enjoy your life!

Resources:

Dr. Robert Young, Author of *'Sick and Tired'* states that 'stress is THE single cause for all diseases; environmental stress being the most underestimated version of it.'

Werner Brandmaier; Geopathic Scientist, Feng Shui Consultant. Institute of Feng Shui and Geopathology

Check out his website: https://www.instituteoffengshui.com

Kathryn Wilking

The Feng Shui Advantage

Appendix D: The PEP QUIZ
This is an extra COPY of the Personal Element Profile Quiz

Every time someone rubs you the wrong way... step back and have a look at the clues. You'll see the element that WILL rub you the wrong way! Smile. You'll know what's really going on.

The more you dive into these elements, I'm sure you'll be as fascinated as I am!

Let's all learn to get along and support each other!

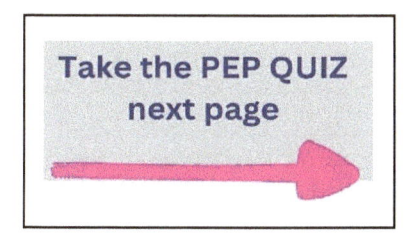

Take the PEP QUIZ next page

Do you know your **_Personal Element Profile_**?
According to Feng Shui, your personality can be related to one of these **Five Elements**. These lists can indicate your strengths in one area or another. Check all that applies to your to find your dominant element! Can you see any friends or coworkers?

WOOD
- Flexible Schedule
- Gets things done quickly
- Loves a challenge
- Goal Oriented
- Can be Impulsive
- Enjoys a change in routine
- Confident
- Thinks BIG
- Impatient; "Get to the point!"
- Likes to wear green

FIRE
- Life of the Party
- Thinks outside the Box
- Takes control of any problem
- Animated and creative
- Relaxed approach to life
- Makes friends easily
- Wide social circle
- Passionate about life
- Drama Queen at times
- Loves to decorate for the holidays

EARTH
- Well grounded
- Reliable and trustworthy
- Happy to Compromise
- Great Nurturer
- Great Mediator
- Asks a lot of Questions
- THE contact for family and friends; the nucleus
- Compiler of people and details/bills/history/facts
- Protective of family
- Likes to wear earth tones

METAL
- Precise thinker
- Sense of Justice
- Speaks UP
- Follows the Rules
- Strong Morals
- Thinks in B&W, no compromising
- Has systems in place; wills/bills/security
- All furniture/objects are squared off neatly
- Sense of humour is lacking
- Does not like to hug

WATER
- Wise, pontificating
- Excels in specialized knowledge
- Very smart and well read
- Seeks the truth, a visionary
- Reflective
- Solitary, loner
- Sly sense of humour; blunt/cruel
- Secretive, private person
- Eccentric, anti-social
- Armchair Traveller

TOTALS

WOOD _____

FIRE _____

EARTH _____

METAL _____

WATER _____

There are no right or wrong answers to this quiz.

The Element with the highest score should be your Dominant Element. Lower scores in other areas will show you have a talent to embrace a wide range of characteristics, which in turn will help make you become a well – rounded individual.

Being a unique character, you have a unique way of getting what you want in this world!

Personal Element Profile (PEP) Quiz copyright Kathryn Wilking Designs.
Evaluations using PEP are solely for the purpose of demonstrating the concepts in this book.
For comprehensive evaluations, please refer to a Certified Feng Shui consultant.
Kathryn Wilking Designs; Your Feng Shui Consultant for Safe and Happy Environments
www.kathrynwilking.com

Author Biography: Kathryn Wilking

**Kathryn is a people person,
adapting with the changing times.**

Kathryn's been working in the decorating business for more than 25 years, and transitioned into Home Staging. When she remarried in 1998, the puzzle was how to blend the two families together. She embraced Feng Shui and used these techniques to create function & flow, and help with the myriad challenges of a new family.

This success sparked Kathryn to learn more, and thus, adapt Feng Shui principles for use throughout her business and personal lifestyle.

As a project consultant, Kathryn has opened, renovated and moved stores and businesses. She offers counsel to blended families and cultivate unique solutions for others to lead productive stress-free lives. Through these multi-faceted experiences, she has observed behavioral as well as design challenges in a wide range of settings. This led to the development of her practical approach, using Feng Shui Personal Elements to promote harmony in any space, home or office.

Now, settled in Ontario, you can find Kathryn out and about: sailing on the high seas, hiking with her husband and collie dogs, travelling around the globe and continuing her spiritual practice with Feng Shui.

Kathryn is eager to share information with all through an informative newsletter each month, blog posts on social media and her podcast Feng Shui Your Day!

Kathryn believes that positive vibes and good intentions are the way to make the world a better place!

More About Kathryn

I've been married to Stephen for more that 20 years.
We are a great team when it comes to home renovations and landscaping.
We recently celebrated the marriage of our son at my new in-law's farmhouse.

Stephen and I have our home on Lake Simcoe in Ontario.
Sometimes, opportunity knocks for us to try something different.
In this photo, we celebrated the summer solstice sunrise with our dogs, in our pajamas!

My hubby and I have Coastal Skipper Certifications and we've been racing small keelboats for decades; this is how we have FUN! I took the helm of this charter as we sailed back along Georgia Strait off the west coast from Saltspring Island to the port in Granville Island, Vancouver.

More About kathrynwilking.com

This is where you'll see me at my desk answering questions and talking with clients. I love to get out to actually see homes and offices, yet, half of my time you'll find me at the desk for virtual consultations.

This is where I record my podcast **Feng Shui Your Day** on Spotify, Apple, I Heart and more.

We love to travel!
I always make an effort to continue to learn more, so I can help others.

Several years ago, I took a Feng Shui tour of Beijing and Shanghai with Jay and Helen James.
Here's a selfie of me with the statue of Kuan Yin in Shanghai.

Many people ask about the origin of my logo. It's a custom designed yin-yang symbol that represents tai chi, good health and balance in life. You'll notice a peacock feather and a single leaf folded into a unique yin-yang ball.

Choosing an auspicious feather or object for a logo can help in business. Peacock tail-feathers have 'eyes' and are associated with greater vision and wisdom. These feathers have been used for both ritual and decorative purposes over the centuries. The iridescent plumage is a blending of five colours (representing the five elements) creating sweet harmony.

You may note notice at first glance, there is a symbol in the lower right corner. It's the Chinese symbol for a horse. The horse is a support of mine personally – I'm a dog in Chinese Horoscope; so this is very significant.

A single leaf is for strength to support a single journey; progressing through life with continuous growth and stamina to rejuvenate and thrive. Feng Shui works in so many ways!

Here's to continued success,

Kathryn

Kathryn Wilking

Happy Clients

Kathryn is very much a professional. I asked her to come over after we experienced a break in. She discovered my home office was of particularity full of negative energy; for years I've had a hard time spending productive time there. As a result, I've remodeled the office (paint and moving the furniture and discarding things) and can say I'm now spending more productive time than before!

My understanding in the work environment, meeting rooms, offices and such all have power positions. Knowing these, I've made a habit of always planting myself in the most powerful position available.
I would highly recommend Kathryn Wilking Designs for an honest evaluation and recommendations based on years of experience.

Thanks, Ken Hembroff, White Rock, BC
~
Dear Kathryn,

Paul and I absolutely LOVED meeting you in person and having the time you so generously gave us and our home! It is such a joy and celebration to connect with a kindred soul, especially when this comes with the great blessing and opportunity to learn and grow from the connection.
Our session on Saturday was the catalyst we needed to break out of our (my!) inertia and get the energy flowing to transform our space and lifestyle. Your presence and guidance are extremely uplifting and inspiring! I am happy to confirm already that we feel a huge shift in our outlook thanks to you!
Thank you for everything you shared with us, for the beautiful, thoughtful gifts, the books and crystals! These are definitely "some of my favourite things" as Oprah would say :)) I started reading your book this morning and I am enjoying it very much!!

The Feng Shui Advantage

Paul and I will digest the overview together and incorporate its direction into planning our upcoming projects. I know there was SO much to retain and provide direction on and I truly appreciate you taking the time to summarize our "mess." Thank you!!

With love and gratitude, Marinela Gheorghe, Ethel, Ontario

~

Kathryn, I would like to thank you for your assistance and participation in the Costco Road Show. It was personally very rewarding to see how hard work pay off. The Costco business model has proven to offer exposure for both beyond our current channels of distribution. As you have found over the last few weeks it seems we continue to have new customers joining the current Josef-Seibel & Romika foot wearers.
Thank you once again for making this a success.
Drew Maternick, Josef-Seibel Shoes Canada Ltd.

~

We hired Kathryn to provide a Feng Shui consultation to improve the energy in our home, for all family members, and to improve our business which we operate from home. Kathryn did some preliminary work prior to the actual in-home consultation and came very prepared.
We made a significant change by switching a bedroom and office. The result is that our son is feeling so much better in his new and private bedroom and is in the "helpful people" area of the home, and our new home office is now located in the wealth and career area of the home, a better location for all concerned. This was the best outcome for our family in making this arrangement.
Kathryn also encouraged us with the placement of crystals for the enhancement of specific areas. Now that we have beautiful crystals throughout our home, we all feel so much better than

Kathryn Wilking

before.

We highly recommend Kathryn for her Feng Shui services. She provides excellent follow-up, explains concepts very clearly, and is a warm and caring individual.

Jane Tennant, Richmond, B.C

~

Dear Kathryn, I just wanted to say, thank you SO much for having me on your podcast and allowing me to share my story with your listeners. It was so much fun chatting with you!

I really appreciate your time and effort in putting together such a fantastic show. You make me feel so comfortable and your questions were awesome!

Thanks again for the opportunity. I hope to stay connected-you rock!

Coach Annie Delray, USA

~

Over the years Kathryn has generously offered a few excellent tips and ideas for my office, so when I decided I wanted to make some changes in my personal life, I asked Kathryn to come to my home for a Feng Shui Consultation. During our initial conversation about my areas of focus, she immediately came up with a number of easy and immediate changes to support those areas. One of Kathryn's great talents is being able to create effective change within your environment utilizing your own beloved furniture and belongings instead of needing to go out and search for, and buy, all new things. Thus far, the results have been dramatic and, more importantly, I enjoy my home so much more.

Jen Wasmund, RAC Acupuncture

Epilogue

When the day is done, it's time to shut down.
Leave the worries and the to-do list at the door.
Grab your favorite beverage, and just be quiet for a few minutes. Look around your space and counting your blessings; a reminder to be grateful for all that is going on in life.

Life continues to change as we grow and maneuver through the journey of life. Will we embrace the ride, or resist change altogether? By looking at things from a bigger perspective, you'll find what's really important.

Love yourself. Love your family. Look down the road with good intentions and positive energy for the future.

When your heart is full, it's so easy to help others along the way. You too, can have a Feng Shui Day, everyday!

Enjoy the ride, *Kathryn*

Kathryn Wilking

Printed in the USA
CPSIA information can be obtained
at www.ICGtesting.com
JSHW070444181123
52081JS00007B/160